RELIGIOUS TEXTS OF THE ORAL TRADITION FROM WESTERN NEW-GUINEA

(*Irian Jaya*)

PART A

RELIGIOUS TEXTS TRANSLATION SERIES

NISABA

VOLUME THREE

E.J. BRILL — LEIDEN — 1975

RELIGIOUS TEXTS OF THE ORAL TRADITION FROM WESTERN NEW-GUINEA

(*Irian Jaya*)

PART A

THE ORIGIN AND SOURCES OF LIFE

COLLECTED AND TRANSLATED BY

FREERK C. KAMMA Ph. D.

E.J. BRILL — LEIDEN — 1975

NISABA is the name of the Sumerian goddess of vegetation and writing, whose symbol is the calamus (the instrument with which the writing was impressed on the soft clay) on an altar. The Sumerians were the first people to use writing, for keeping accounts and, by extension, inter alia, as a substitute for the oral tradition. For this reason, the goddess has been given pride of place here.

ISBN 90 04 04391 8

PRINTED IN BELGIUM

CONTENTS

PREFACE

It seems desirable to render a brief account how and when these texts were collected, so that the reader may know something about the collector, translator and commentator.

Still in Holland, I studied the situation in New Guinea (especially Sentani) from 1929-1931 and then went to Hollandia-Sentani-Genyem, but stayed there only for a few months. In 1932 we moved to Manokwari and started to learn the Numforese-Biak language. Then in 1933 we settled down in Sorong (immigration area of the Biak-Numforese), learned the Moi-language and culture, and had nearly finished the investigation when world war II ended the first period in 1942. All the texts collected, field-notes on the Moi and Betew (Biak immigrants) were confiscated and afterwards all burnt. Some of the most valuable notes we took with us in the prison-camps, but in vain : these shamanistic drawings were suspect and confiscated also.

About the shamanistic drawings and systems two publications appeared just before the war (1939, 1941-42). More about them is to follow. So about 150 texts (80 Moi, others Biak, Betew, etc) were all lost. After the war (1948-'54) I studied cultural anthropology at the university of Leyden under the guidance of the late Professor J. P. B. de Josselin de Jong. In 1952 during some months additional material was collected in Biak and Sorong, in order to complete my thesis Ph. D. in cultural anthropology, which was achieved in 1954. (Translation in English : "Koréri, the Messianic movements in the Biak-Numfor culture area" then with additional data up to 1972).

After 1954 we went back once more and stayed in the field until the end of 1962. My main task was missionary work, but in the mean-time I did field research wherever possible using the two languages mentioned already and the lingua franca Indonesian.

The greatest stumblingblock for every fieldworker is the great variety of languages and cultures. In the Sorong area alone there were about 15. We now lived in Hollandia, making long trips into the field and got the possibility, later on the task, to do researchwork among the Sentani-Skow-Sarmi river Tor, Sawar-Bagaiserwar; Japen, Sorong (Moi) and the Tehit, Mejbrat in the Birds-Head peninsula. Once more our collection of texts multiplied, not least with the assistance of my friend P. C. Bothoff, Director of the Teachers Training College, who put at my disposal the texts collected by his students; I. S. Kijne had a great number of texts alas most of them in the Windesi and Wandamen language. From the late F. J. F. van Hasselt I inherited Numforese and Swandirbu texts, written by P. Wandow, J. Rumbruren, P. Rumbekwan. Very greatful am I to K. W. Galis Ph. D, D. Griffioen from South New-Guinea, and not least to Jac. Hoogerbrugge who gave permission to quote from his booklet about Sentani. Of the unpublished collections I made use to complete an all-round picture. Many times I had to use the medium of the Indonesian language, an unavoidable medium and a great help in this multilingual country.

As a great many of texts are at my disposal I could check the texts by way of comparison. The most characteristic ones were selected and given in a somewhat artificial scheme. But we are aware of the negative aspects of this method. For texts should be given in the context of their cultures. In order to cope with these difficulties we tried to give in the notes as much data as possible and mentioned in the bibliography the available publications dealing with these cultures.

This was at least a possibility to save these texts from oblivion, for there are already too many lost forever, or "burried" in unknown corners as "unpublished fieldnotes" : inheritances from former times.

We aim to give these texts in at least three volumes. The first one : "Origin and sources of life", the second one : "The Threat to Life and the Defence of Life", and the third one about the Birds Head Peninsula : concerning the Moi, Tehit and Mejbrat, in the context of their culture in brief.

The first text from Southern Irian I translated, as it is a remarkable specimen about the origin of earth and men, while most tribes take the creation of the earth for granted, whereas they elaborate about the coming into existence of men, animals, rivers, the sea, lakes, bays etc.

I tried to translate as near as possible to the original texts, and the result must be a more or less clumsy English or at least stiff and sometimes seeming lifeless. Without the help of my friends H. J. van der Poll and his wife (he lived in South Africa and the U.S.) I hardly could have succeeded. I am very thankful to both of them and also to Mrs. Van Baaren, who gave the whole her finishing touch. Now and then it must have been "a firm grip".

Simon Kooyman Ph. D. was so kind as to read the introduction critically and his suggestions were most valuable.

B. A. van Proosdij Ph. D. gave directives concerning the selection and the translation of the texts. It goes without saying that I have to thank many friends and colleagues but also that the whole responsibility for the composition, the notes and the translation rests upon my own shoulders since in most cases I translated directly from one of the Irianese or Indonesian language, however some texts were translated into the Dutch language. I nevertheless hope the "sparks of the mythical reality from the past" will come to life again and enflame and brighten our insight in the most remarkable world of the ' hidden language".

The titles of the myths I brought in accordance with the context, in order to make this clear from the very onset and an index superfluous. Originally the myth only bears the name of the most important personality operating in the narrative. Sometimes the texts are named as follows : tale about the first human beings, or : about the origin of fire, the moon etc. I selected the most complete ones and had to leave out many variants, but not always. Sometimes these variants were necessary to explain how people living in each other's vicinity nevertheless have quite different ideas about the same important happenings. Compare for instance the notes about the first text.

A feeling of independency is always present even in the most deeply rooted conviction. Variations are as many as dialects present and therefore these tales are seldom boring, embedded in the local culture they give a lively descriptions of cultural reality.

F.C.K.

BIBLIOGRAPHY

1955 Adatrechtbundel, Part XLV, Kon. Inst. v. Taal- Land- en Volkenkunde : Nieuw-Guinea. Den Haag.

1966 Baal, J. van, DEMA (Description and analysis of Marind-Anim culture, South New-Guinea). The Hague.

1971 Baal, J. van, Symbols for communication (An introduction to the anthropological study of religion). Assen.

1915 Balen, J. A. Windèsische verhalen (Bijdragen Kon. Inst.). Den Haag.

1953 Bidney, David, The concept of myth, in : Theoretical Anthropology. New-York.

1974 Castaneda, C., Journey to Ixtlan (lessons from Don Juan). New-York.

1974 Droogers, André, De gevaarlijke reis (The dangerous voyage-initiation of boys among the Wagenia in Zaire). Thesis, Meppel.

1962 Evans-Pritchard, E.E., Social Anthropology and other Essays. New-York.

1955 Galis, K.W., Papoea's van de Humboldtbaai. Thesis, Den Haag.

1956 Galis, K.W., Sociografische notities betreffende het Sentanigebied, Gouv. Ned. Nw. Guinea, no. 24. Hollandia.

1957 Galis, K.W., Ethnografische notities over het Sengge-gebied (Onderafd. Hollandia), id., no. 86. Hollandia.

1957 Galis, K.W., Ethnologische Survey van het Jafi district, id., no. 102. Hollandia.

1930 Halie. N., Het hoofdenvraagstuk in N.O. Nw. Guinea, Bijdr. Taal- Land- en Volkenkunde 86, no. 2.

1888 Hasselt, J.L., Gedenkboek van een 25-jarig Zendelingsleven op Nieuw-Guinea (1862-1887). Utrecht.

1947 Hasselt, J.L. en F.J.F., Noemfoorsch Woordenboek. Amsterdam.

1942 Held, G.J., Woordenlijst v. h. Waropens, Ned. Nw. Guinea, Verhandel. v. h. Kon. Bat. Gen. van Kunsten en Wetenschappen, Dl. LXXVII, 2e stuk. Bandoeng.

1947 Held, G.J., Papoea's van Waropen. Leiden.

1957 Papua's of Waropen. Den Haag.

1956 Held, G.J., Waropense teksten, Geelv. Baai, N. Nw. Guinea. Den Haag.

1967 Hoogerbrugge, Jac., Sentanimeer, Mythe en Ornament, Dl. 9 van : Cultuurpatronen, Bulletin Ethnogr. Museum. Delft.

1974 Ilogu, E.C.O., Christian Ethics in an African background. Leiden.

1929 Josselin de Jong, J.P.B., De oorsprong van den goddelijken bedrieger, Meded. Kon. Ac. v. Ws. Afd. Letterkunde, dl 68, serie B. Amsterdam.

1937 Josselin de Jong, J.P.B., Oraita, a Timorese settlement on Kisar. Amsterdam.

1939 Kamma, F.C., Levend Heidendom (shamanism), Meded. Tijd, Zendingswss. 83. Oegstgeest.

1942 Kamma, F.C., Kringloop en burchten (shamanism), Tijdschr. Opwekker. Soerabaja/Bandoeng.

1954 Kamma, F.C., De Messiaanse Koréri-bewegingen in het Biaks-Noemfoors cultuurgebied. Thesis, Den Haag.

1972 Kamma, F.C., Koréri (translation of thesis in English, and up to date facts added). Den Haag.

1956 Kamma, F.C., De Sentaniërs-local survey. (Typescript).

1961 Kamma, F.C., De Sentaniërs en de Humb. Baai dorpen, in : Memorie van Overgave (Transfer), betreffende Hollandia, J. J. W. Dubois, Gouv. Ned. Nw. Guinea. Hollandia.

1970 Leach, Edmond, Lévy Strauss. London.

1955 Lévy-Strauss, Cl., Tristes Tropiques. Paris.

1962 Lévy-Strauss, Cl., La Pensée Sauvage. Paris.

1932 Locher, G.W., The serpent in the Kwakiutl religion. Leyden.

1973 Locher, G.W., Claude Lévy-Strauss, in : Filosofen van de 20e eeuw, Bertels C. P. en Petersma. Assen/Amsterdam.

1941 Nevermann, Hans, Ein Besuch bei Steinzeitmenschen. Stuttgart.

1973 Saliba, John A. Myth and Religious Man, in : Missiology, an international Review, Vol. l. Juli.

1946 Schuurman, C.J. Er was eens .. er is nog (inleiding in de sprookjes-wereld, fairy-tales). Leiden.

1961 Vries, J. de, Forschungsgeschichte der Mythologie. München.

1928 Wirz, P., Beitrag zur Ethnologie der Sentanier, Nova Guinea 16. Leiden.

1929 Wirz, P., Bei liebenswürdigen Wilden in Neu-Guinea. Stuttgart.

1931 Wirz, P., Die totemistischen und sozialen Systeme in Holländisch Neu-Guinea, in : Tijd. Bat. Gen. 71.

1933 Wirz, P., Am See von Sentani, in : Ned. Indië Oud en Nieuw. Amsterdam.

INTRODUCTION

"Plusieurs choses certaines sont contradites, plusieurs fausses passent sans contradictions; ni la contrediction n'est marque de fausseté, ni l'incontradiction n'est marque de verité."

Blaise Pascal : Pensées

1. *Myth : religion and reality*

Because of the difference between the two phenomena, world-and tribal 'religions', it seems necessary to explain why in this series of religious texts attention is asked for *oral* tradition too.

The greatest difference seems to be the form and the process by which the transference to the succeeding generations took and still takes place.

But more important is the fact that oral traditions, shaped into the myths, are always on the move along with the culture of a community in a given time and place.

Therefore the dynamic character of the myths is always manifest, as a diachronic investigation will show. This time-perspective is mostly due to a certain kind of acculturation. In order to cope with the ever-changing circumstances, situations, contacts, myth avoids fixation and termination, its character is flexability.

The method is rather reformulation, instead of the interpretation or re-interpretation usually applied for the texts of the world religions. One of my informants from the Humboldtbay made this point very clear to me in his rather worrying remark : "In putting down our myths and legislative rules in writing you just kill them". He meant to say : "To fixate or stabilize a progressing living reality means to cut it off from accompanying the living community". As will be shown in our oral texts the society accepts new elements and names and gives (in the Myths) account of the changing situations, but (and this is important) by way of a strict traditional system or scheme.

But the most important feature of the oral texts is the fact that they are concerned with an undifferentiated totality and wholeness. The specific religious elements cannot be singled out without damaging this totality, and the same holds good for every aspect of the culture. The three main aspects (religious, social and economic) are interdependent. In our texts we see clearly the "mixing-up" of all aspects of culture. This only *seems* to be confusing, for this reality embraces life as a whole, it is a complex in which the heart of the community beats the rythm.

And this religious aspect of the tribal cultures is the justification and the reason why myths of the oral traditions may be called religious texts (cf. also : G. W. Locher : 1932/7).

We suggest therefore the following definition : Myths are religious convictions laid down in dramatic expressions and symbols limited by tradition, which determine and accompany the community."

Why *religious* conviction or "truth" ? (cf. J. van Baal 1966 : 205, "Myths are religious truth in story-form").

Because it is a fact that religion presupposes the supernatural reality and in the minds of the people under discussion here this reality is all-embracing, the physical as well as the metaphysical (the physical counterpart of reality is regarded as the revelation of the supernatural life-power).

Therefore we encounter here an undifferentiated reality, including matter and mind terrestrial as well as superterrestrial existence, heaven and earth, the living (and this is very important) the dead, the ancestors. "It is religion which gives to culture ultimate orientation and direction" (E. C. O. Ilogu 1974:9).

In this world-view limits and boundaries are (at least in the tales) neglected, and this view of the "universe" (taken in the most literal meaning of the word) is mirrored in the main aspects of culture, but especially in the myths and in the rituals corresponding with them.

Another crucial problem in the myths is the specific form and metaphors applied. They seem and are indeed sometimes absurd, trivial and abhorrent as nightmares.

After our first thorough contacts and investigation in the field (1931-1942) we tried to explain this in the following statement : "The stories and tales about supernatural reality are deliberately given in dramas contradicting the normal terrestrial sequence of events, causes and effects in nature and human life. To grasp reality in its totality the people here do not rely upon or attempt very profound reasoning resulting in formulas, on the contrary. Myths tell us about impossibilities, illogical happenings, in order to draw attention to the fact that they are, by this means, pointing to the supernatural, numinous reality." Twenty years later I found my description of the world-view under discussion most clearly expressed by E. E. Evans-Pritchard (1962:179), where he states :

> "...the very improbabilities, even absurdities in many myths are not to be taken literally, and hence as naivity and credulity, *but are the essence of myth, which just because the events lie outside human experiences, demands an act of will and imagination*" (italics FCK).

Another problem, however, we have to face is the fairy-tale element. In the Numforese language two different words are used : kakofen (fairy tale) and kakaik (myth). The first category consists of animals who behave like human beings, they talk, use tricks and deceive eachother. They have nearly always an aetiological character, but they are sometimes part of a myth, and these fairy-tale parts are told to children and uninitiated and often to strangers (cf. our texts A2 and note). J. van Baal in his important voluminous study "Dema" (1966) states :

"...there are only few Marind who are good tellers of myths. Not everybody among them is interested in mythology. Very often they only tell a fragment ... selecting just that part which, for some reason or other, take their fancy at that particular moment" (ibid. : 206).

And more clearly yet :

"Often the people themselves do not have separate terms for story and myth. Whether the story is a myth or just a story has to be decided from the attitudes of storyteller and listener. Even that is not always a reliable criterion. It often happens that myths are told to the field-worker without any proof that the relater believes his stories to be myths, that is, religious truth" (ibid. : 205).

From all this we may conclude : there are in reality neither clearcut entities nor complexes of tales simply named myths and others fairy-tales.

Some psychologists even go so far as to annex the fairy-tales to the realm of myth, be it a special kind of myth.

C. J. Schuurman, 1946, said :

"Fairy-tales give an independent account or translation of a mythical consciousness, but they have a character of their own and are therefore to be regarded as a special form of myths." (1946:16)

This statement would certainly not have been agreed to by the cultural anthropologists some years ago. Nowadays one is not so sure anymore. The experience of Van Baal (1966:205-208) seems to me commonly agreed upon. He states :

"In some situations the distinction between myth and story dealing with the supernatural loses a great deal of its applicability, both are expressions of the people's experience of something supernatural" (1966:206).

Scientifically speaking myth is man-made, but it is an *answer* or reaction to an ultimate supernatural reality recognized and believed in by man all over the world. This religious consciousness is a fact sometimes even a compelling force which urges human beings to answer.

This answer can be given in dramatized form (myths) and this form may be analyzed in a scientific way.

The answer can be given in a more or less dogmatic way too, and is as such liable to criticism, but the *ultimate reality* escapes strict formulation and is as such-sui generis-inaccessible.

Baffled by the story-tellers and sometimes, after having learned the language used, deeply struck by the remarkable meaning in these tales, it may not be surprising we learn to visualize as the people involved do, and to feel what they mean.

We are enabled to voice this "hidden meaning" after having grasped the general attitude of the informants and their people.

Though having to converse in Spanish (a strange tongue for both of them) C. Castaneda tried to perform this miracle and laid in the mouth of his informant, Juan Matus, a Yaqui Indian sorcerer the following world-view, which holds true for the Papuans (Irianese) as well :

> "For me the world is weird because it is stupendous, awesome, mysterious, unfathomable..." (1974:81).

2. *World-view and universe*

While writing this title down I hesitate, for we must avoid the impression of an existing, clear-cut ontology or cosmology. Theoretical interest seldom seems to be the cause of consideration, but does exist. J. P. B. de Josselin de Jong once stated (1937:167) :

> "...archaic cosmology is never in the first place popular cosmography, essentially it is not popular cosmography at all, the latter element being always a by-product, the fairy-element in the myth" (instead of "not popular" we should prefer : "no cosmography" K.).

In my thesis (1954, English in 1972) I wrote :

> "What is curious about the myths is not that they have been composed but that they are believed. Belief, though depends on the existence of a specific tradition. Every myth must contain a point of contact for identification. Not everything is believed or suitable for being handed over to later generations. A mythology without a system would be chaotic, it would not provide an acceptable basis for society" (Kamma, 1972 : 65).

Besides the questionmark which has to be put about the "not being curious of the composition", another very important problem arises, namely : whether the system (Levy Strauss would say *structure*) is deliberately structured while it forms the basis and gives a special shape to the way-of-thought.

Exactly formulated and clear statements are rare, but nevertheless they do exist. But are these systems, concepts or structures unconsciously present ? Many answer are given in the course of time.

These explanations of the myths and tales during more than 2500 years show nearly every aspect of this remarkable phenomenon.

From the explanation of Euhemeros the Greek philosopher (mythical dramatis personae were once historical persons) up to Levy-Strauss with his so called structuralism (mythology is based on an unconsious structure) is a far cry indeed. And it seems to me that, concerning the just mentioned basic statement, Van Baal (1971:212) has rightly raised the question : " ... how unconscious is the unconscious ?". And :

> "Levy-Strauss over-emphazises the part of the unconscious and neglects the contributions of culture and conscious life. Actually the notion of the unconscious is a dangerous notion, which ought to be tabooed. As a reification of the laws governing man's spiritual life, the notion of the unconscious necessarily leads to mystifications. It did so with Jung, up to an extent it does so to day even with Levy-Strauss".

To this clear statement may be added the consideration whether structuralism does not lead us dangerously near again to the road of Levy Bruhl, who impressed the scholars in the years after World War I, with his "mentalité primitive". According to Locher however Levy-Strauss denies this danger" : myths are no product of prelogical thinking" as Levy-Bruhl concluded (Locher 1973:205).

Our personal opinion has considerably changed by communication in the "field" and even more after the study of the texts of the Bird's Head Peninsula of New-Guinea (Irian). I was most strongly impressed by the discovery of the meaning of the secret men's societies. Being initiated into the secrets of three different societies (the Kambik of the Moi-people, the Jewon of the Tehit and the Samu-Won of the Mejbrat) I had to take an oath to keep these secrets. From 1960 until 1974 I did so, but in the year last mentioned I got permission to disclose and publish what is behind the curtain. We intend to do so in the Nisaba series, in our third contribution. Important for us is now what appeared to be the core, the very heart of these secrets as the informants put it, namely : "We use symbols for the children and women (and strangers, K.) but only the initiated know the real meaning of these symbols".

Remarkable is the fact that in his thesis concerning the

boys' initiation among the Wagenia of Kisangani (Zaire) André Droogers concludes :

> "Culture is taken to mean the capacity of man to use symbols to structure his way of life. The order thus created is only seemingly constant. Symbolic structures make man, but man also makes symbolic structures. Though man is subject to his culture, and accepts large parts of it without asking questions, he is also able to change the symbolic structures, changing the symbols, or the structures, or both.
>
> The Wagenia initiation is an example of this position of man as *agens* and *patiens* of symbol systems, ordering and reordering symbols" (1974:278).

Holding in mind the above-mentioned fact we are led to the assumption "the real world-view of the inhabitants consists of the conscious use of symbols, and these symbols point to a supernatural reality, the ultimate power".

Only what is believed stimulates to action in accordance with this conviction. Therefore one finds in nearly every myth and often in folktales also indications and explanations about the position of, and even more about the functions which a member of a group is obliged to perform. This not only holds good for the more ritualistic, but for the practical and even more the political activities as well.

Bearing in mind the ultimate foundation always explained and eagerly elaborated on, we may perhaps put the question whether" profane activities as such" do really exist and if everything is not embedded in religious consciousness. This assumption is not meant to lead to the conclusion that we meet here with the so-called "eastern mentality in which religion plays a dominant part". It is much more the point of departure and here we encounter the following (systematized) features of the world-view of the Biak-Numforese in the first place :

1. Life-Power incorporated in the arch of the sky, called Manseren Nangi (The Lord Sky or Firmament).

2. Life is derived from the ultimate life-power and reveals itself in a great variety.
3. One of these varieties is the human being, who lives by the grace of nank (mana).
4. Some human beings are specially gifted and this charismatic quality they owe to Nangi. Sometimes this quality is inherited and derived from the uaropo (spirits) (: *ascribed status*, very important among the Sentani-people) others achieve this quality by their deeds (: *achieved status*, more important in the Geelvinkbay area).
5. Man gets the feeling of being on the same level as every living creature, animals and everything that grows and eventually dies included.

Impressed by the geographic surrounding, awed by the natural phenomena it seems impossible to him that all this exists and happens without an intention. Man himself experiences the birth of children, the growth to maturity and the unavoidable old age and decline of strength ending in death. All this man has in common with animals and trees, plants etc. Every living being and even strangely shaped rocks and impressive mountains and hills, every being, every thing came into existence. Once upon a time they were not yet there.

Therefore every life, to begin with, must be a revelation of the one and ultimate and overwhelming life-power. There are only quantitative and hardly qualitative differences, but everything has its own place, relation and function within a homogeneous group and a specific system is the foundation of such groups. All these groups together form the universal totality.

But neither the system nor the structure means life. They are only the backbone and taken for granted. No "primitive" man is systemridden, this seems to be the privilege and even the joy of the outsider who really is able to discover more systems and structures than the people involved are aware of, but he is at the same time not able to live or give life within the limits of the structures he discovers or builds.

And let it be clear from the very start : myths form a hidden language. During about 2500 years students have been baffled by this phenomemon and have tried to solve the" hidden problems and offered "the key" to the real background problem. And yet, despite of the many different solutions, nearly everyone of them (cf. J. de Vries 1961, about the history of the investigation concerning myths), I repeat : nearly everyone sometimes hit the mark, at least marginal.

Indeed we are reminded at Goethes sentence : "Viel Irrtum und ein Bischen Wahrheit" (Faust). But the remarkable fact remains that neither a student nor an especially gifted "fact-finder" has ever succeeded in putting together these truth-elements into an acceptable general and overall picture.

D. Bidney once wrote :"

"The great myths are those to which moderns ascribe an implicit, or latent, symbolic truth-value which may never have been intended by their originators.

The great myths lend themselves to a variety of symbolic interpretations, and their greatness lies precisely in their prolific suggestiveness for the creative imagination of the sensitive artist" (1953: 301).

And the ideas and suggestions of the students were as prolific as the imaginations of the originators, and even more so as they were not under control of a close-knit and well-integrated community. Bidney warns against this kind of mythology :

"I am inclined ... to the view that there is no one single symbolic interpretation of a given myth which is the correct one and that all attempts at a monistic, "scientific" mythology designed to reduce all myths to a single type are bound to be discredited eventually. In their attempt to rationalize the symbolic significance of ancient myths, philosophers, theologians, ethnologists, folklorists and psychologists have sought for a single type of reality or a single type of truth underlying the variety of mythological expressions and thereby have only succeeded in inventing" scientific" myths of their own" (Bidney 1953:302).

I am inclined to the view that the people involved know a great deal more about backgroundsystems and structures than the Western scholars are prepared to admit thus far.

It would be a curious thing concerning myth, if the people themselves were the only ones not to understand the backbone of their own myth structure.

This must be a wrong conclusion, as I am sure the future will show or even prove. My personal experience I already mentioned, Droogers conclusions from Africa are another proof. That these should be the only ones seems impossible.

The Papuans (Irianese) however are aware of the fact that their tales when taken literally make no sense, but feeling sometimes themselves unable or unwilling (it may even be taboo), to explain the background to strangers, time and again the informants will say or write : "Of course this is nonsense of our ancestors, they were stupid". I left these evaluations out of the texts, but at least 1/4 of the writings of the pupils of the teacher training college, marked B. S., made this remark or something like it. Sometimes, and even very often at the borders of the different tribes, melodies, dances, songs, names etc. are borrowed or bought. As a member of a jury on the occasion of a dance-show by different tribes in Sentani, I discovered that even 2/3 of the performances were not of their own traditional stock, hence neither meaning of the words they sang, nor that of the adornments was exactly known. The same applies to the songs I heard from the Biak people. Of course there were many original Biak, but some were borrowed or bought from the island of Japen (Sup Arwa as they name it) or even from the Island of Mapia.

This made translation nearly impossible and comment on the songs also.

3. *Cosmological features in the world-view*

The use of the word "cosmology" has to be understood as being rather inductive than deductive. Terms like philosophy and ontology presuppose an intentional or premeditated aim i.e. a theory in which contradictions are avoided in order to obtain a more or less closed system of thought.

But the people concerned are in no way interested in such a theoretical thought-system.

What they want though is a suitable explanation. This nearly always concerns practical matters, events that occur and phenomena experienced or witnessed.

Sometimes this will lead onto a completely wrong track, as far as truth and reality is concerned. For instance the principle : post hoc, ergo propter hoc.

Nevertheless some main lines may be sketched.

In rough outlines we may state that the experience of man has led him to the assumption of an apparently strong dualism, it may even be characterized as "a dialectical attitude of mind" deduced from the phenomena in nature and human life-experiences. The well-known principle of cosmic dualism is one of its features.

Voiced by the shamanistic practitioners, though hardly by the common members of the groups concerned the Biak immigrants in the Raja-Empat area assume two complementary realms :

1. *The world of the wind* (dunia wam; dunia=world; wam=wind). The meaning is: the invisible, supernatural, spiritual realm and the concept of the holy.
2. *The world of the body* (dunia baken; baken=body). The meaning is the visible objects, matter.

With his body a man is a part of the second, with his soul, his life, he is part of the first one.

The dunia-baken forms the limit, the borderline within which the dunia wam lives and moves and is sometimes within reach of the humans, but mostly beyond their life and hands. In the myths however these borderlines are often neglected. This possibility points to a primeval state and situation in which the totality of these two worlds still existed. Neither had division taken place between "wam" and "baken" "heaven and earth" nor were the human beings scattered and dispersed over the surface of this earth. Terrestrial dwelling-places were not yet determined as nowadays. The term "primeval" is used in many texts. The myth therefore recalls and brings to mind that time in which the most essential events in human existence and in the cosmos took place. Therefore myths belong essentially to a sacred sphere, but they do not remain in the primeval time to give a picture of that time only.

One of the remarkable features is exactly that they form a continuing stream, adopting foreign elements, absorbing or explaining everything important, but at the same time colouring these new elements, transforming them so that they fit into the total picture and the character of the original traditional themes. It is therefore that the time-perspective, the diachronic features are of great importance, as they often caused the differences and variations of the same myth.

4. *The stratification of the universe*

The geographic situation (mountains, caves, and the like) is often reflected in the world-view of the people concerned. Around the Sentani-lake area and the coastal villages the mighty mountain Dafonsero (on the maps named Cyclops) dominates the whole landscape. Relatively spoken not very high (about 3000 meters, just as high as the Arfak-mountain near the bay of Doré (Manokwari) but very impressive because the Davonsero stands an isolated giant and mirrors his shape in the surface of lake Sentani, or has clouds whirling around his top.

The layers of the universe as seen by the Sentani people are therefore threefold. The upperworld, resting on top of the mountains, the human world (the terrestrial abode from the bottom of the lake to the top of mount Davonsero) and the underworld.

In the Geelvinkbay area four layers are mentioned and drawn by the shamanistic medicine-men in the Raja Empat area (Sorong).

1. *The Sky* (*Nangi*), the abode of Manseren Nangi, but more exactly Lord or God Sky, the starry arch of the firmament which is so impressive in clear nights during the period when the moon is dark. Man is at such times conscious of the universe and all its mysteries stooping down over him. The Lord Sky (Mans(e)ren Nangi) is worshipped as the high-God, and oaths are taken at such times with the introduction by a leading old man : "Hi, brethren, the sky is very near, our oath will be powerful now". It is told and drawn that the souls of those decapitated have gone astray and at last found a dwelling-place in the Milky Way. Their shapes are not unlike

the "life-symbol" (anch) in the hieroglyphs of the old Egyptians.

2. *The world of the clouds* (*Mandep*). This layer consists of the worlds and the spheres of the four main wind quarters, each one with his own over-Lord, here named Korano (king, chief). The Eastern and the Northern wind-Lords are well-disposed or benign towards men, but the other two harbour malignant spirits. West and South are inhabited by evil and adverse powers as far as mankind is concerned. Therefore the starry Sky and the world of the winds (clouds) are also the abode of the Great Evil, the Korano Faknik (Lord of the evil spirits).

3. *The earth of man* (dunia snonkaku). The terrestrial surface divided into land(sup) and sea(swan), living-place of man in his first earthly life. But this earth is also the battlefield of the supernatural powers, mentioned sub 2. The aim of these malignant powers seems to be the destroying of human beings and stealing away their souls.

4. *The underworld* (jenaibu) abode of the dead. This location includes different spots and has different names accordingly.

4a. The inside of the earth (among the Birds Head Tribes : the tops of mountains and even hills). The gates to the abode of the dead are the caves, deep wells and high trees, among others the banyan. The way to the bowels of the earth is found inside the trunk and the roots.

4b. The bottom of the sea. The gate here is formed by the caves on small islands, especially Numfor, Meosbefondi and the islet Entsjau (Kaju Puluh), near Jayapura. On Meosbefondi is a deep well. The dead peoples, souls emerge every now and then to the surface, and sit on the beach of the islet, hence the name : jèn (beach, sand) aibu (the dead). Different islands and mountains are named, even among the same tribe. It seems as if the inhabitants of each village have separate dwellingplaces for their dead as well. Sometimes a general term and the indication : land or abode of the dead is named in the texts.

But the inside of the earth is not only the dwellingplace of the ancestors and the dead, but also the source of rejuvinating energy. Everything growing comes from the inside of the earth, therefore she is the source of life and the ultimate dwelling-place for man : eternity is there.

5. *The geographic-and the mythical East and West*

According to the opinions of nearly all the inhabitants of Irian (Western New Guinea) the horizon, the sky-line in the far East and the far West forms the connection between heaven (the sky) and earth. In the East the life-giving powers have their abode and the sun gets the opportunity to arise out of the embrace of the night and the underworld, but only with the assistance of dwarfs with a turning-wheel does he succeed.

To be sure there is the possibility of a fifth stratum here : the world of darkness underneath the terrestrial surface which is of course flat. This is meant when "underworld" is mentioned, when the sun and death are concerned.

For the West is the location of the gate to this underworld. It is the residence of the dangerous Lord of the Western wind as well, and therefore the source of the Western storm-monsoon. The gales and high waves with their thundering breakers and surfs pounding the reefs and beaches are impressive and threatening indeed. The difference between the geographic and mythical West however is noteworthy. The first mentioned contains a challenge to the navigators in their big seagoing and seaworthy canoes, but at the same time the journey to the West is "the dangerous and perilous way of every life". One hardly forgets that the West is the realm of death as the East is the origin of life.

Hence when East or West are mentioned in a narrative it does not always mean the geographic West or East, but often "the life journey".

6. *The symbolic meaning of the animals in the myths*

We have seen already that an animal is one of the expositions in which life reveals and expresses itself.

Most of the tales concerning the primeval age give the clear impression that human beings and animals were not yet separated and accordingly there was not yet a fundamental difference between the two categories of living beings. I.e. human beings were able to metamorphose themselves into the disguise of an animal and the reverse. But : not all animals could serve this purpose. Mostly the animals chosen are very familiar to the people and even frightening e.g. the crocodiles and big snakes.

In the second part of our oral religious texts in Nisaba we will try to give a more extensive account of this topic, especially concerning the snake and/or dragon. A few remarks may suffice here. Sometimes the metamorphosis is a kind of disguise intentionally accomplished to try the minds and intentions and the characters of people involved in the tale as well.

It seems that in some tales there is an arising consciousness of a kind of evolutionary process. For instance the sequence : banyan-tree; animals, human beings. However, reverse events and regressive powers are at work at the same time, i.e. it often happens that human beings are transformed and metamorphosed into animals. The myths of the great floods later on will show this fact more clearly.

The point concerning the disguise often seems a kind of moral or ethical and educational lesson: Those who rely on their eyesight only are bound to be deceived and disappointed. Reality is in fact not always what it looks like. Behind the overt appearance is always the covered, disguised reality.

Remarkable : it is nearly always the youngest and most humble one of several sisters, or a child who recognizes this" hidden reality". The most dreadful appearance often harbours a noble character and the ideal human being, and this one becomes the giver of life and wealth. The demarcation-lines between the species of living beings are not strictly drawn, hence the two of them are used as symbols presenting an even more hidden reality. It is the human task to chose, and his choice appeared in the myths nearly always determinant for the future of mankind and world.

SECTION A

THE CREATION OF EARTH AND MAN[1]

A1. *The tale of Kutaiwakerémi*[2]

In times immemorial land did not yet exist. There were only the sea and the air. Birds flying in the air were not yet there, nor animals living in the sea.

There lived in the sea only two shrimps, a big and a small one, which were able to change themselves into men who could make land and sea. They could make animals, fishes and birds too.

Tefafu (the deity Kutaiwakarémi, whose name it is usually avoided to pronounce) alone cannot make human beings. He only cares for them and looks after them from their youth until maturity, and until there are many of them and the earth is crowded with men.

The two shrimps that live at the bottom of the sea, the big and the small one, changed themselves into human beings and became father and son. The name of the father is Tefafu.

The father and the son went to the surface of the sea to have a look at the situation there. They saw no land only sea, much water but no dry land at all.

So they went back to the bottom of the sea in order to take ground from there. They took some and swam to the surface again in order to make dry earth there. They laid that ground on the surface of the sea, went back to the bottom and then again to the surface to see what had happened with the bit of ground they had placed there. Then they saw that this ground became larger all by itself. Then by itself there came much dry land, the earth and rivers and oceans too. At that time there where not yet trees and living beings on that dry land.

All by itself there came a house, in which father and son took their abode. Nothing grew yet, nor trees. Then Tefafu urinated on the land and on that spot a tobacco-plant grew. This plant grew very well, became bigher and bore fruit. Tafafu took these fruits and planted them. All by itself every kind of tree grew from these fruits, until the dry land grew full of them.

Father Tefafu and his son lived near the Jawibusu river, a tributary of the river Chochi. This is the area of the Jair-people near Tagiob.

Living there they met another Tefafu with two of his sons. The Tefafu with his two sons arose from the earth. According to his own explanation he owned two children, two sons.

Tefafu who came out of the sea is very powerful, but the Tefafu out of the earth is not able to make anything.

(Nevertheless) the sea-Tefafu and the land-Tefafu became good friends and they lived near the river Jawibusu, the place where the clan Mumuchagi is living now.

As the sea-Tefafu is much more powerful than the land-Tefafu, he commanded the other Tefafu to take care of the three children. He himself made a trip all over the earth in order to find out whether there was (somewhere) a place to go and live. He saw everything he had made and it looked very good.

He also found a place to live in, namely there where the sun rises.

After that he went back to his namesake with the three children, to the river Jawibusu. When he arrived at the other Tefafu's place he found out that his own son, who came out of the water too, had died. Only the two children of the earth-Tefafu were still alive. Therefore the water-Tefafu called upon the earth-Tefafu to part with one child, to replace his dead son.

The earth-Tefafu (however) did not agree, he refused to give one of his sons to replace the deceased child of the sea-Tefafu. This was the reason why the friendship between the two Tefafus chilled. At that very moment they did not understand each other's language any more and they separated.

When the sea-Tefafu's child died he made the earth-Tefafu promise him to take his corpse with him wherever he should go. And, if ever the sea-Tefafu should become angry and come home, the land-Tefafu should not be obliged to tell the father of the deceased son (in case he should have forgotten it) about the promise once made.

And so it happened after the separation between the two Tefafus. The two children of the earth-Tefafu remained where they were and (their father) took the corpse of the sea-Tefafu's son along with him when he left for the place where the sun sets. His own children stayed behind.

The sea-Tefafu also went away. He took the direction to where the sun rises and he did not take anything with him.

The two children of the earth-Tefafu stayed near the Jawibusu river. Later on they disappeared and became the owners of the area near that river. Therefore until now the people (living) there pay homage to that spot and are still afraid of it. Once a year or so the people of the Numuchagi-clan offer a sacrifice on that (historical) place.

Tefafu of the earth went to the West, to the place where the sun sets and remained there. "His offspring multiplied and is coming back now much more powerful than we are. Their name is Chochi[3] (Jair-language) or Kwai (Kombay-language). They come to administer us (coming from the sea) or they bring the Gospel".

The descendants of the sea-Tefafu are the perfect ones, they are the people of the Jair and the Kombay, because they are descended from the perfect Tefafu.

People with another skin colour and straight hair descend from the imperfect Tefafu, who went to the West with the corpse of the child of the perfect Tefafu.

Tefafu of the sea who went to the east, to the place where the sun rises, did not walk always straight on. He crossed the whole area from the Jairs and the Kombays, until he grew (became) old and arrived at the border of the tribe-area.

Nowadays he lives at a place bearing the name of Vamini, a tributary of the Kasuari river which in its turn is a big tributary of the Digul river. That is the place of the Wiwo-bunachujocho clan. This clan gets orders directly from Tefafu and passes them on to other clans. Tefafu remains all by himself in the place Vamini, nobody accompanies him.

On a certain day he walked along the river Vamini and he heard a child crying. He went in the direction of that noise and saw there a boy and a girl.

He asked the two whence they came and where their mother was. They answered : "We dont know where we come from and we have no mother. The only thing we know is we came out of the eggs of a lizard. Our mother is a lizard".

Tefafu took the two children and took care of them until they became big and strong.

To the boy he gave the name Adama, and the girl he named Efama.

From these two all human beings are descended, after a

very long time. But these people were really not yet perfect. They were very disobedient, they had a big scrotum, very big ears and their skin was scaly and they didn't give honor to Tefafu. Tefafu himself saw clearly that these people were not in conformity with his own appearance.

Therefore he took two children, a boy and a girl and put the two in a bamboo-tube. Then he destroyed the whole of mankind by fire and after the fire with water, which covered the whole dry earth. The two children in their bamboo-tube drifted away on the big flood (water).

When the earth became dry again the two came out of their tube and multiplied until there were many people (again).

All this happened three times, while man was still not yet perfect. Only after three times (of catastrophe and rebirth) Tefafu saw this kind of people were now perfect.

These perfect ones multiplied until there were very many. The Jairs and the Kombays are descendants of those perfect people.

Tefafu now nominated representatives of the tribes in order to represent them. Each clan has its own representative. Nowadays Tefafu is only sleeping.[4] He does not walk hither and thither any more. He does not stand (on his feet), he does not sit down, he is only sleeping.

When there happens to be an earthquake it is caused by the fact that Tefafu turns himself over on his other side. A small trembling of the earth means Tefafu is lifting his head.

When he turns himself over from left to right and back again this will cause a big earthquake.

If Tefafu were to be roused up and walk the whole earth would be destroyed and all life wiped out, all the animals would die. Therefore sacrifices must always be brought to his representatives. But the sacrifices are only allowed if Tefafu himself will ask for them by means of his representatives. The people ask these representatives what kind of sacrifices are wanted. If Tefafu asks for an entire pig, people will bring the animal, still living, to the place where sacrifices are usually delivered. They put their heirlooms[5] on top of the sacrifices and kill the animal with arrows.

A child of about 12-14 years of age is allowed to shoot. Only a man who has never committed adultery is allowed to shoot. After the killing the pig is cut into pieces and then the people have to wait a moment until a bird gives a cry or a fly comes and settles on the meat. This is a token that Tefafu has accepted the sacrifice. No women nor small children are allowed to be present. The men present will eat the pork, mostly mixed with sago. The bones of the pig are disposed on the same spot and left there, only the heirlooms are taken back home.

After the ceremony is over the men make a joyful outcry and leave (for their homes).

The spirits of the deceased ancestors have their abode in the invisible world. Every human being posesses two souls. The souls of the deceased go to Tefafu.

One soul goes back to the invisible world, whilst the other goes to Tefafu.[6]

A2. *The banyan-tree, the source of life*[7]

As told by our ancestors and passed on from generation to generation of "*the history of the ancient country*".

My parents told me and they said : Our ancient country, the land of Biak grew in the following way : In the beginning there was land, but there were no trees as many as now.

There was, to be exact, only one single tree to be found, namely the Banyan(asarknam). Only this tree was there but he grew abundantly and became very big (and tall). His leaves and branches extended and gave a marvellous shadow.

Out of this banyan tree all other trees sprouted and all kind of animals originated (of his trunk and branches).

The narrative mentioned runs as follows : The chief-clan (ER) at the beginning was born of the two animals the crocodile and the iguana. The crocodile was a man and the iguana was a woman. My parents told me : We saw them and they looked like animals, but the two of them were in reality human beings. They, the two of them, gave birth to us.

On a certain day they, the two, quarreled about a certain object, namely a triton's shell (kbur).

The woman (the iguana) said she wanted the shell so that if it should happen that the children, boys and girls should start to cry and weep, she could blow on the triton's shell so that her husband the crocodile would get the message that something was wrong at home.

But the man i.q. the crocodile said : he wanted to possess the shell to be able, after they had made a raid and killed people to blow the shell going back home. His wife and their children when they heard it could be sure of the home-coming of their husband and father with great joy.

In this manner the two quarreled over the shell for a long time until the woman (the iguana) took hold of the body of the shell and the man (the crocodile) seized the rim and then the two started to pull to and fro. At the time they pulled that shell they metamorphosed themselves into a man and a woman (Insren Nangi) of great beauty, yes they had the likeness of heavenly beings, Then the woman started to cry and weep, but the man did not yield and his grip on the shell was and remained powerful.

When the struggle went on and on, a snake (metamorphosed into a human male) started to talk to the struggling partners, but the snake in his appearance was like an animal, but he really was a human male of a marvellous appearance and his heart was longing for that woman, so he talked to sweeten and soften her heart saying : "It is much better you let go the shell and your husband owns the triton, because he is a man. Then he will be able when he comes home after a succesful raid, having killed many people in war, to blow the shell and then we all know this at once when we hear its sound".

In this manner the snake talked a long time to the iguana and he softened her heart and diverted her attention from the pulling. Diverted in this way she slackened her grip on the shell. The crocodile at once took advantage of her attitude and with a mighty pull he took the triton's shell and made for the sea where he dived into the waves with his prize.

And this result caused the fact that now we only find the triton's shell in the sea. When we take a living triton home we always remark a mucus secretion from the living triton. These are, according to the narrative, the tears of the woman. At the mouth of the shell we clearly see until this day the pawmarks of the crocodile, while on the opposite side the signs of the smaller paws of the iguana are visible. (These are the signs of the prince Crocodile and the princess Iguana).

The woman was so angry at the snake, who diverted her attention by his "sweet talk" that she cursed the snake, so he has no "feet" as other animals have. Among the snakes there were some who wanted to go to the sea in order to regain the triton's shell from the sea or the reefs, and give the shell back to the angry woman (iguana) to appease her anger and get her forgiveness. But when they arrived on the reefs the crocodile had already made an agreement with the octopus to meet the snakes and talk to them.

But the "negotiation" meant war and an attack was made at once, when the octopus discharged his "ink" and blinded the eyes of the snakes so they could not find their way back to the shore. This fact drove the snakes to recognize the octopus as their chief and they begged a place to live in. So they honoured him and stayed in the sea. At first the octopus wanted them to stay near, but afterwards he nominated the jep-snake (the biggest one) as chief of the seasnakes and made them live in the deep sea where near the reefs the depth is black, another kind of snake, the karabas and the adef could live and remain on the reefs wherever they wanted.

On the day peace was achieved they agreed to call each other nephew (napirem : fabroso).

But the snakes living in the sea with their headman were afraid the promise made to each other by the two partners would not be strong enough, therefore they asked with great politeness if the octopus would talk with the crocodile in order to persuade him to give a real token of friendship to them.

So the octopus and the crocodile agreed and they gave the following sign (token) : The crocodile and his grandchildren should never wage a war against them in the sea, but the other animals on the earth should do that always. And after that he promised to take care that the octopus and his grandchildren never should forget this agreement. Kais, the octopus as the king of the sea gave a real sign namely : He gave one of his tentacles to Jèp and he ate it and he swallowed it as a sign (of his goodwill) and then they called one another napirman (fabroso).

The first delegates of the snake clan did not come back, therefore the snakes living on the continent ordered another delegation to the sea-snakes. One of this delegation rose and said : "In a few moments I will go, but please rub my body (with oil) till it shines and becomes smooth and slippery in order that nobody will be able to get hold at my body". Thus they rubbed his body until it became very slippery and then he started and went in the direction of the sea.

At that time they met their brothers (now seasnakes) and they told them about everything that had happened and they enjoyed it and heard they had not in mind to go back to the land. Therefore the new delegation too wanted to stay, because the life in the sea was obviously much better than on the shore. They had their chief there, the great Kais and he was a creature with much patience, and he was able to live in deep waters but on the surface too. And there was his friend the clan crocodile, a hero. And they too were able to live in the sea and on the land. These were the reasons why the second delegation did not go back either. Therefore they got the name Sakon (they stayed too) for they stayed to live in the sea.

Some time later they decided to make an agreement with the iguana, in order that she and the landsnakes should acknowledge them if they were to dwell in a river. But they were afraid of the big landsnakes, therefore they persuaded the iguana to discuss the situation with them in the river. And so it happened. This was the manner in which the Wonggor (crocodil) Kasip (iguana) and Kais (octopus) got the possibility to live in the sea, the rivers and on the surface.

And so they did, but concerning the frog, he stole life from the water saying he too wanted to raise himself in order to be of importance on the land also. But this resulted in making all the animals from the land very angry so they tried ever since to get hold of the frogs and eat them. This is the reason why the frogs always scream at the top of their voices.

This happening caused all our parents to warn their kids most strongly against stealing saying : "Everbody who steals and gives his children to eat thereof, he will not only be ashamed but grow also very thin and his back will become humpy just like the back of the frog (mangroder) or the thief".

The iguana after she lost her quarrel with the crocodile, jumped back to the hills. There she beats with her right paw under the arm-pit of her left one. This caused a remarkable sound. People heard this sound and decided to take as the skin of their drums the hide of the iguana. So the drum became the voice of the primeval mother, their ancestor mother. The men took as their sign the triton's shell, which is blown in all important situations : the coming back from a succesful raid, the gathering of people on the occasion of an important ritual.

The Wonggor, the crocodile, was used as a sign of war, the name of heroes and to frighten everyone who does not agree with the wishes and custom of the clans involved. Not everyone is allowed to bear this name, nor use the crocodile as a decorating motive on the stem of his proa / canoe. It is even more dangerous, because the crocodile will take revenge on people who are infringing the rules. They have to ask permission of the clans involved first, and if they reach an agreement they may use the crocodile motives in their woodcarving. In former days our ancestors took care of and fed the crocodiles and they commanded the crocodile to punish the trespassers and evildoers, and their enemies (cf. the notes about the fairy-tale element in this myth).

A3. *Mangundi the creator of the Numfor people*[8]

In the well-known myth of Mangundi which is told in many different versions, the Numfor people elaborate on the miracles he performed. These were very important to them because they claimed to be created by this mythical hero. Here we select those parts of the myth as told by the clan Rumfabe from Numfor, in later times the pioneers who moved to Doré, centre of the missionwork since 1855. The informant himself, writing in his old age, has once been a well-known Evangelist in the service of the Mission. His version is therefore the more remarkable and he starts with a kind of general confession concerning the creation of man (cf. notes).

Text. In the beginning, in primeval times Allah[9] created heaven and earth. Together with everything and everyone, human beings included, which are found and live on earth, or are in command of the earth, is created by Allah. This means every nation white and black living and dwelling on the shores and mountains.

But we, the Numfor-people according to the information of Sawari (Rumfabe) owe our existance to Mangundi. He and his people were created in primeval time and his name was Manserenba (no-Lord).[10] on the island Biak.

(The writer then elaborates on all important events : the poor state in which the old man, a widower lived, the meeting with a being out of the "underworld", his long journey to the East, arrival at Meok Wundi and the encounter with the morning-star metamorphosed into a human being, whom he caught while he was stealing the palm-wine of "the old man".)

While Manserenba was hiding himself in order to get hold of the thief of his precious palm-wine he heard a noise as if a certain object was bursting amid the shining light of the morning-star Sampari. The old man terrified by the light and the noise nevertheless caught this heavenly being and said : "So it was you that troubled me all the time, who stole the harvest of my garden and now you are stealing my palm-wine. I am not going to turn you loose". Then Sampari became frightened because in a few moments the sun would rise and that would mean his death. So he gave a piece of wood to the old man with the words! "I will explain to you how to use this piece of wood. You just make everything you want and you will get it. This piece of wood will become to you as a tree of life. When you become hungry, just knock on something and you will get plenty of foodstuff, everything you like, even the most miraculous things".

But Manserenba did not yield, so the heavenly being promised him "knock with this piece of wood on the sideboards of a dugout and the canoe will travel all by itself". No result, the old man seemed to be most stubborn, so Sampari said: "Whenever you should like to get a woman to marry, just throw the fruit of the Bintangur-tree[11] and you will succeed". After this last promise the old man turned the morning-star loose and tried to practice what Sampari taught him.

He climbed into a Bintangur tree, picked one of its fruits and prayed : "O, Lord Sky (Manseren Nangi) if you really elected me to become Lord in this country, I will throw this Bintangur-fruit and everything Sampari promised me will come true".

After this prayer he threw the fruit, hit a maiden and she became pregnant. Her relatives discovered what was going on and when after the birth of a son, Konori, it was found out that the old man was the father, they destroyed the village and moved away, leaving the young mother and child, her brother and her husband behind and went to the island of Jappen.

Having neither food nor water the situation became critical. The old man Manserenba, got his promises from the Morningstar, in reality he had become Manseren Mangundi (the Lord Himself), but his appearance was still in bad shape. His whole skin was covered with scabies and sores and no wonder that his wife despised him. When after three days they became hungry and the child Konori cried for food, his mother Ningai said to him : "Ask food from your father, can't he give you his scabies as food ?".

Konori went to his father and passed on the words his mother said unto him. Then Mangundi realised his magical power he could rely upon. So he said to his son : "Come into my room and have a good look". Thus Konori entered the room and lo, the room was filled with every kind of food they needed. He told his mother about the miracle his father had performed ; at first she did not believe it, but then she too went to have a look. She saw the abundance of food, and they ate as much as they could but there remained more than they could eat. After they finished their meal the food-remains vanished. Mangundi himself did not know what hunger was, so he did not join them at their meal.

Each day Mangundi performed the same food-miracle, until his wife, the young Ningai became bored and she said to Mangundi : "Why didn't you perform this miracle while our people were still here with us. Then they would certainly not have left us". And after that she complained about the fact that she had neither company, nor relatives near to talk with and she said : "Why don't we take a dugout (wai=canoe) and join our relatives in the South, where they must dwell now if you are really as mighty as you pretend"? Mangundi, ashamed by these words, went to the beach where the debris of destroyed dugouts still were. Then he put together some parts of a demolished dugout and prayed saying : "O, Yes Lord Sky, if you really nominated me as Manseren Mangundi, I will strike this remains with my magic piece of wood in order to make a new canoe". Than he did as he had said and lo, a new dugout was created out of the debris. Then he went home, told his wife, her brother and his son about the proa ready and complete on the beach.

They were amazed but gathered everything they could take into the canoe and embarked at once. No crew was there anyway, so Mangundi prayed again : "O, Manseren Nangi if you really made me Manseren I will embark and the canoe will travel all by itself". And so it happened. The canoe was running at high speed in a southerly direction steered by Mangundi.

Then the son woke up, and cried because he had no place to play. Therefore Mangundi told his brother in law Saneraro : "Cast anchor". This was done and, lo, an island rose out of the sea, the boy went ashore, played as he liked and they gave the new island the name of Meos Indi. After the boy had played enough they embarked once again; the same event took place a few moments later. So the island of Aibay came into being. They made progress to the south and arrived at a small rocky island; there the boy once more cried, because he wanted a place to play on. The small island bore the name Numfor. After constant howling of his son Mangundi just stepped over board and walked on the surface of the sea and everywhere he went the sea became solid ground and a remarkably beautiful island came into existence. It was named Poiru (rise up), but in later days they applied the name of the small island Numfor to the new island, (Numfor : the holy-island) The small island is still there, seawards of the village Pakriki.

Mangundi now felt his own personal appearance did not fit any more in the appropriate conditions just created, hence he again applied his magical power entrusted to him, but not without the assistance of the High God. Therefore he prayed once more : "Yes, O, Lord Sky (Manseren Nangi), if you really raised me to be a Manseren let me demand this ironwood tree to become a great fire". At the very moment Mangundi said the words, lo, the irontree was ablaze. For the second time Mangundi now prayed with the same words : "Yeah, Manseren Nangi if indeed it was you who created everything now existing on earth, I beg you Lord to let me throw myself into the fire in order to be able to complete all our intentions. And let my body (my skin) be transformed into all kinds of valuables : antique china, textiles and the like".

At that very moment he threw himself into the blazing fire, so that his old skin was burned completely. And the moment the old skin fell off it really was transformed into everything valuable in the world. His own appearance had changed entirely. His complexion was now of a marvelous quality and he was like a young and strong man. He now wanted to decorate his body. He prayed to the Lord Sky, in the same words as we have heard already, and asked for a mirror, to be able to see what he looked like. He then got a big shell (tridacna, or chama gigas) and started with his first experiment. He took a pair of trousers, a shirt and shoes, and looked in his "mirror" (the shell filled with water), but did not like what he saw. Then he tried to dress himself as a moslem, with a long white robe and a turban, but did not like this either when he saw himself in the "mirror". (fanin). At last he tried the customary way : clad with a loincloth of a treebark named marbin, and after that decorated his body with all kinds of "jewelry" : bracelets of beads and shells on his arms and legs, a wonderful shell for his forehead and a comb in his hair decorated with the crest of a crested pigeon. He then mirrored himself and enjoyed the sight and he said : "This is really what I wanted to be"; he only added the tailfeathers, black and white coloured, to the comb and now it was a real asis mambri (comb of the hero). He was now ready to face everything to come. Contemplating his new appearance and wanting to impress his young wife, brother-in-law and his son, he prayed again but the content was different. He prayed : "O, Lord Sky, if Thou indeed created me in order to become Lord grant me a cannon that it may become clear that Thou hast elected me to become king of Papualand". And so he got his big gun. Than Mangundi ordered his cannon" : Hi, cannon, fire". And the cannon fired all by itself and the first boom of the big gun echoed with a thundering roar.

After all this happened Mangundi went back to their dwelling-place and left the hill Orkersbari. When he returned home he walked on the large reefs, because it was low-tide. His son saw him coming and recognized his father at once, but his mother could not believe her eyes and she said : "That man coming is quite another person than your father". But the son was right. He arrived, went into his room and placed there all his valuables he had gained from his old skin; then invited his son to have a look. It was overwhelming what the boy saw. Already impressed by the boom of the cannon and the complete metamorphosis of his father he now shouted from sheer joy. At first his mother was hesitating, then full of admiration and joy, the more so as on the veranda the sirih and pinang and betelnut[12] awaited her in a bowl made of silver (papon sarak).[13] So they all lived in peace.

But not long after that famous day the woman started to complain again, because she had no relatives and friends around to show them their treasures (robenei) and to talk with. Day after day Mangundi heard her complaint, but he kept silent.

Then on a certain night he did not sleep, but was watching the stars. He now had to perform his greatest miracle and therefore he waited until Sampari, the morning-star rose. He took his bow and arrows, went out of the house and stood in front of it. Then he prayed : "Yeah, Lord Sky (Manseren Nangi) if it is really true you made me a Lord, create from these four arrows which I am going to plant in the earth, four clan-houses crowded with human beings".

After this prayer he stabbed the first arrow in the ground. and lo, a clan-house arose from the soil and Mangundi named it Numberpon (Rumberpon : the first house). Then he tried the second arrow and the second house appeared which he gave the name Rumansra (the house where they eat coconut). The third one came and received the name Angeradifu (at the feet of the limetree), the last one made its appearance and was therefore called Rumberpur (the last house).

When the first people of the Numberpon were created, they came into being, but they still lived in the dark. This means they were not yet able to talk properly. They spoke but what they said were unintelligible utterances, but the second house and the next ones already spoke much better because they were dwelling in the light. The place were they lived became a village and it was named Pakriki (the solid one).

This village became in the long run so crowded that Mangundi's wife said she became afraid. Her husband answered : "How is this possible, you begged and complained until all these people were created, now you start again and feel ill at ease".

The Numfor people had their anxiety too : they had no food at all.

There was a female Infadwarni (the trouble-maker) of the subclan Rumbekwán,[14] and notwithstanding the fact that they had lived for quite a long time on the food-abundance made by Mangundi's magic stick, she was worried about the uncertainty of life. One day she saw smoke arising at the foot of the mountains of the island of Arwa (Jappen) in the South-East direction, and she shouted to the men : "Hi, you, have a look. Smoke is rising from the island of Arwa. Are you still sleeping. Much better you men make some canoes and take food from the Arwa people."

The men obviously approved for they made for the forest. Mangundi tried to stop them saying : "Please wait a few moments and see what will happen". But the men refused to listen and headed for the forest, and though Mangundi said : "If you really want to start just lay your tools at the foot of the trees and then come home again", they went and started to cut the trees and came home in the evening (very tired). When the next morning they wanted to finish their work Mangundi said to them : "If you really want to go again, just lay the axes and hatchets on top of the trees you have cut down already and then come home". But again the men refused to do as Mangundi told them. So the whole day they labored hard, shaping the trees in the canoe-form and dug out the canoe's. Nobody had ever made a canoe, therefore each group of men tried to do it according to their own imagination. They made the canoes ready : after the hollowing out, and the shaping of the outside they attached the outriggers and the "floaters". Then they wanted to pull the canoe to the beach but in vain : the many trees blocked their way so they made no headway at all. Only the clan Rumfabe did the job in the right way : They hauled the body of the canoe easily between the trees to the beach. There they attached the outriggers and floaters and built a small cabin on top in the middle of the canoe.

After having finished everything they went with these first canoes in the direction of the island Arwa, as they were told by the woman Infadwarndi.

After that on a certain day a child of the clan Rumbekwain fell ill, and the parents and relatives started to cry, which Mangundi had warned them not to do in such cases.[15]

Now Mangundi arranged a meeting of all the people present. He told them : "Everything I prohibited you you just did".

1. I forbade you to go to the island of Arwa from where the smoke of fires arose. But you started to build canoes to sail to Arwa.
2. I forbade you to cut the trees, then to dig them out, but you did the reverse.
3. I forbade you to wail if somebody should fall ill, but you did not act according to my words.

The results you have already experienced : You have to work with all your strength and with only a small reward (result), and all of you will experience death. That is why I am going to leave you. So Mangundi embarked with his wife, his son and brother-in-law. Then they just vanished;

their house and belongings disappeared and only some remnants are left behind. (i.e. On the rocky cape of Orkersbari at the island of Poiru, now named Numfor). There is the place and the cold embers of the fire in which long ago Mangundi burned himself to a new life and body. The big stone with a hole in it, this was once the anchor of Mangundi's canoe and next to this piece of rock one can find a long piece of rock having an opening. This was once the cannon used by Mangundi.[16]

At the time the Numfor people, left behind by Mangundi, just remained where they were, there was a great silence, but then somebody said to the multitude of people : "Now look in what kind of situation we have brought ourselves. When our chief Mangundi was still here, he took command over our lives and all was well. Now just have a look and see. Who is guilty of this situation?". Then the people started to discuss what was said and they agreed that the woman Infadwarni Rumbekwan was the great culprit. All of them became very angry with her, but nothing could be changed at the moment.

They only hoped that one day Mangundi would come back to his homeland in order to start a time of abundance once again.

After about eight years they were stirred by the two men Sawari Rumfabe and Bari Rumbruren. They had seen the white clouds surrounding a black massif which must be land. They agreed upon that.

So they divined (kinsor[17]) and the result confirmed their conclusion. Then they prepared their canoe for the first big journey. Some of our ancestors said, the people wanted to go westward in order to follow and maybe to find the dwelling-place of Mangundi. They meditated and divined once more before they left the beach of Numfor in the direction of Doré. They arrived in the beautiful bay. (They did not find Mangundi there, but in later days they erected a temple, Rumsram,[18] in his honour and their people settled there, however most of them spread along the East Coast of the Birds Head, and some of them from the clan Rumberpon went to the far West and chose as their dwelling-place some islets (Jefman etc.).

A4. *The origin of the Numfor-Interior people*[19]

In primeval times, even before the Biak people settled on the South-coast under their leader Mangundi, the Numfor-Interior people came into being and dwelled in the midst of the island.

In those primeval times there existed two chief-clans namely the Kawyan and the Kamér. They came into being as follows. In times immemorial there was in the middle of the island a single banana tree. On a certain day this banana-tree was felled and out of its trunk came a human being, a male who was named Kawyan. This Kawyan became the ancestor of the (afterwards named) old-Numforese. Kawyan was a proud male of high rank (a real Manseren).[20]

He got children and this offspring multiplied rapidly, so in the course of time there were a great number of them. They became the origin of the Numforese-Interior.

At that time they branched off into different sub-clans. The first clan got two subclans : Kawyan-Yewun and Kamér. These two main clans divided into two and the other into three branches. So Kawyan had two sub-sub-clans : 1. Rum Kawyan and 2. Rum Jewun. Kamér got : 1. Rum Kamér; 2. Rum Sér and 3. Rum Miak.

All these people dwelled near the sources of the rivers. They elected Kawyan Yewun as their chief or king. His clan had therefore the right to rule the whole island, and Kawyan Yewun became their leader (and hero : mambri) in raids and combat.

At that time these Numforese-Interior (or Old-Numforese) dwelled exclusively in the interior. They were afraid to go to the beach. If somebody accidentally was near the sea and he heard and saw the surf on the reefs, he ran back to the woods.

Once it happened that a dog ran to the beach. There he met people, who were living in the village Menukwari (the old village). The village chief Dimarakwar Angradifu understood what that dog meant namely : there are other people living in the interior. He wanted to contact them and so with food and fish he lured the animal to come near. He then bound round the neck of the dog some fishbones and let him go home.

The Numforese-Interior heard of the dog returned to his master (owner) and understood what the fish round the dog's neck meant to say. One of their chiefs Yewun Beba went in the direction of the beach, trying to locate the beach-people. He succeeded and made friendly contacts with them. He discussed the situation with Dimarakwar and the result was that beach-and interior-people communicated freely with each other, they fraternized and even intermarried. But in the long run the friendship did not last. They argued, even killed each other and this meant war.

This fighting and killing between the coastal and the mountain-people resulted in a victory of the latter. Hence the coast Numforese left the island in great numbers. Some of them resettled in Rumberpon, Roon, Doré, Amberbaken and even in the Kolano Fat Islands (Raja Ampatgroup).

At the same time in Biak war broke out between the different groups and this resulted too in many migrations and a dispersion of the Numfor and Biak-people all over the Geelvinkbay and the Western parts of the mainland. This must have happened in the 16th century.

At the same time a big fleet and army from the West, from Gém (Gébé, Dyailolo (Halmaheira) and Sup Rain (Island of Ceram) invaded Papualand, killed and took as prisoners thousands of the inhabitants and conquered an extensive area. The captured Papuans were kept as slaves (in the Molucca-Islands Tidore and Ternate) and had to work in those far-away places. The same fleet came as far as Numfor and killed many people, but this raid ended there too. The "great chief" Yewun Beba, descended from the famous chief and bearing the same name, formed a great army and defeated the invaders by killing their commander with a bone-tipped arrow. The invaders had to retreat to their own country and Numfor was liberated from the enemy and the people lived in peace.

(After this encounter with a fleet from the West, it is most probably that the Numforese-Interior build their village on the coast. The first village was Kaméri, the next ones Warido and Menukwari. The people must have learned how to build canoes and how to fish, this becomes clear from the following legendary history.)

On a certain day Yewun Beba arranged a big fleet of war-canoes and headed Westward along the coast (of the so-called Birds Head). In the middle of the sea, near Kolano Fat they discovered an even bigger fleet of Halmahera, bound for the Eastern parts of the main land and islands.

The commander of the Halmahera fleet ordered his men to open fire upon Yewun Beba's fleet. Then Yewun arose, stood upright with his bow and arrows. The commander of the enemy aimed his shotgun at Yewun, who shot a split second earlier. The commander of Halmahera was struck numb while the arrow was shot exactly into the barrel of his gun. This meant the end of the whole fighting and the two partners agreed in making peace then and there. Their agreement included reciprocal help. The two commanders exchanged their fishing strings (cord). Yewun's cord named Kasuari was given in exchange for the cord called Farimamfarwar (in order to see the end). Halmahera's commander gave his mast, consisting of one piece and got back a mast formed of three slim trunklets. In this manner the two enemies became friends and the Numforese lived in peace again.

(After this succesful outcome of a dangerous situation, Kawyan must have made far-reaching plans. He must have made the long, apparently honourful journey to the Sultan of Tidore, in order to get a title, after having offered his tribute : birds of paradise, slaves, amber and turtle-shell. But even more to get the "blessing" of the — in the eyes of the Papuans — "great monarch" : the Sultan of Tidore. The Papuans firmly believed in his supernatural power, his Nank(a) of which power the visitors got their share, because it was granted to them to kneel before the Sultan and to touch his feet. The chiefs then got their title, sometimes a flag of Tidore too, but the common "sailors" of the tribute-offering chiefs, got only this supernatural power, in Indonesian (Arabic) called" barakas". The above-mentioned sequence of events must have taken place, because our informant, after having elaborated on the coming of the Biak people to the Island Numfor, mentioned the chiefs of the Numfor-Interior and the Kawyan-chief entitled Sengaji.)

At that time there were different great chiefs commanding the whole of Numfor which was divided into four parts, divisions.

1. Sengaji Kawyan, great Chief I; Yewun Beba, Great Chief II.
2. Sengaji Rumsaro in command over the Pakriki area (East).
3. Dimara Meosrifu commanding West-Numfor.
4. Sengaji Berengkes Rumansra commanding East Numfor.

(This is the end of the history of the Numfor-Interior until the time mentioned. Gradually, step by step they got more mana, their chiefs performed famous deeds, even miracles.)

A5. *The female Kangaroo* (*Amori*) (*mother of multitudes*)[21]

A married couple from Windesi rowed (paddled) to build a canoe at Wanduni. When they had cut enough (for that day) they lay down and cohabited. In the late evening they went home and then the female kangaroo came and lapped the sperm from the place where the couple had lain. The next day the two came paddling again, did the same as the day before, and after their work the couple slept together and the Amori came and repeated what she did the day before. This went on for several days until Amori (became pregnant) gave birth to a real human being, a son.

The wife from Windesi also bore a son, it happened in the same way for the two of them. Amori stayed in the forest with her child until it was grown up. Then the boy went to the beach trying to catch some fish. Amori remained in the woods. The boy caught fish until the flood tide, then he returned to his mother. The boy roasted the fish, he gave some to his mother and they ate together. After their meal they slept until morning and waited until the tide was low, then the boy went to the beach and the reefs and fished again. When the flood came he went home and they prepared the fish, ate it and went to sleep until daylight. This day the mother and son went together to the beach, the mother sat on the sand of the beach and the boy went fishing.

At that time the Windesi people went to the South, trying to catch some fish. In the evening they went home and told their relatives about the boy they saw coming out of the forest, fishing.

They asked each other who he could be, but it was evident it was not one of them. Therefore they decided to go again the next morning and to lie in wait to see if he should come again.

So they did and that morning the boy with his mother came indeed. She remained on the beach keeping watch over the arrows of her son. At that moment the raid left their hiding-place and attacked the boy who was fishing. Some of the attackers tried to get him from the seaside, others from the direction of the woods, but the boy shot at them and they fled. But then came the third band and he had to surrender. They brought him to Windesi and brought him to his real father. And so he and his brother, the son of the Windesi woman, grew op together until they became adults.

They agreed to make raids near and far away and so they attacked villages of the Fak, Manekion, Syari, Wariab (and all the coastal villages) even Meoswar, Roon, Wandammen, Waropen, beach-and forest-people. During these raids Sisinjori, Amori's son captured two slaves and Maniwori only one. And so it went on and on. Always Sisinjori caught and killed more people than his brother Maniwori. Coming home the village people honoured Amori's son more than Maniwori. This made Maniwori very angry.

On a certain day they prepared to make a raid again. So Maniwori said to Sisinjori : we will go to the island of Numfor, and they went to the island. Here as always Sisinjori was more brave and lucky than Maniwori. He captured ten slaves and the latter only one.Exhausted after the fighting they fell asleep on the beach and Sisinjori slept like a log. This gave Maniwori the opportunity he waited for. The crew brought Sisinjori's sleepingmat, blanket, headrest, bow and arrows and laid his belongings by his side, then they left him behind and returned home.

When the womenfolk in the village of Windesi heard the sound of the triton's shell, they understood that the two brothers were coming home victoriously as always. But then they heard the sad tale, that Sisinjori was dead, killed in battle and this time he captured only one slave while Maniwori this time had ten.

When Sisinjori awoke, he saw that he was left alone by his brother and the crew of their canoe. Het said into himself : "My brother has lied to me and has cheated me. They have left me behind". When his mother Amori heard the reports of the homecoming men, she was very sad and wept.

She took a number of cucumbers and used them as a necklace, jumped into the sea and started to swim whilst weeping saying : "Amori stringed cucumbers as a necklace, she is swimming in the ocean, in what direction she will float"?

She swam along the coast until Oranswari, then she swam to the East until she came in the area of the island Numfor, where she swam along the beach until she arrived at cape Inaryori. Very tired she clung to the rocks of that cape, and her fingerprints are still to be seen there. After that she went to the shore and climbed on the beach. Weeping she walked through the island seeking her son. Her son slept when she wept and he heard her voice. Then he rose and was angry with his mother saying : You Satan, bad old woman, why do you cry ?".

And the mother said : "I went to seek you, because your brother says. 'The Numforese have shot you dead' ". Then Sisinjori said : "He belied me, when I slept on the beach as a log, they left me behind".

When the two of them had said all they had to say, the mother said to her son : "Come to me, cut me into pieces".

The son answered : "What should become of me if I did what you want me to do ?" But the mother insisted and repeated her words once more now saying : "Cut me into pieces, but do it carefully. Be careful with my head, my heart, my spine and my sacred bone, lay these ones in a separate place, and after that cut the greater part of my body into small pieces, and go and distribute them according to the number of tree-trunks you see here around us".

And so the son started to do what his mother ordered. He took her head, her heart, spine and sacred bone and laid them in the middle of the place. After that he distributed her body in small pieces according to the number of tree-trunks, each tree got a piece of the same size.

That night the son slept until the morning. He woke, saw what he had done and sprang to his feet. He stamped with his feet saying : "This village, hi, are you still sleeping.

Arise and let us fight our battle". And lo : At that moment there they stood, all of them and everything out of the body of his mother the kangaroo : People in multitude, houses, canoes. And his mother (who was metamorphosed into a real human being) and he had the big house in the middle of the great village.

After that they prepared the canoes, and they rowed (paddled) with about one hunderd vessels. They rowed to the West to Windesi. And as soon as they arrived there they fought (and defeated) the Windesi-people.

After having finished the fighting, they left for the East, and there, on the island of Numfor they remained (for good).

A6. *Uri and Pasai and creatures on land and in the sea*[22]

Uri and Pasai[23] are the two men, who were close friends. They trusted one another (and that feature in their characters resulted in the most strange and rare events time and again). Uri was thin but very tall, as tall as a mountain. Pasai, on the contrary was fat and only as tall as a tree.

On a certain day Uri said to Pasai the following words : "My dear and wise friend, please grant me a favour and let your friendly heart agree with my request that means on this occasion : 'Let us make snares in the sea and on the shore' ". And the answer whole-heartedly given was : "Alright".

The next morning the two friends started and went to the forest where they wanted to gather some materials, such as rattan and the like. When they were ready with the collection of materials they walked back to the beach to discuss the shape of the snares. Most difficult was the problem with the snares in the sea, because just that morning the surf was pounding the reefs and beach with great force.

The two friends thinking deeply (about their problem) saw no possibility (for the snares in such a kind of waves). Than Uri said as follows : "My friend, it is much better that the two of us direct our thinking towards the invention of a good tool to catch fish in the sea, what about a trap of bamboo ?". Pasai answered : "All right".

And not long after that they made ready a great many traps and snares to use in the forest too.

This done they distributed traps and snares. Uri got the traps to lay at appropriate places in the sea and Pasai got the snares for the forest. After this sharing each of them took his job. Pasai made the snares fit under some big trees, places where great animals like pigs, deer, elephants, cows and other animals took their way. In the same way Uri was active on the reefs and beaches. He sank his traps in deep places (near the reefs). Having finished their job (task) the two went home.

The next morning Uri walked to have a look at the snares of his friend, after he had inspected his traps where he saw nothing at all had been trapped. But he was greatly amazed when he saw the snares of his brother. No single one which had not caught its prey. Uri considered deeply about what he had seen. His conclusion was no other but this : He must remove and catch all the big animals out of his brother's snares, to wit : elephants, pigs and dogs, and put them into his own traps in the sea. After two days the two friends went to have a look at their snares and traps. First the two investigated Pasai's catchingtools, the snares, but nothing at all was to be seen, no single snare had caught a prey. After that the two made for the sea to have a look at Uri's traps along the beach.

They arrived at the beach and behold : the sea was very

muddy (and in the beginning they saw nothing in the troubled sea-water).

When they saw this they hoped for a satisfactory catch. And this hope was indeed not in vain.

They started to pull the first trap and they got an elephant inside it. In the second trap they found a cow and the contents of the third one was a pig, but alas the (rattan) rope snapped (and the traps went to pieces). And the same happened with the fourth trap which had a horse in it and the fifth, where a dog was trapped.

(But the two brothers) continued to pull ashore thousands of traps with all the (big and small) animals living (now) on the shore (and in the forests). Only three (in reality five) traps were snapped, and went to pieces.

From times immemorial until our recent days, we still are able to find the remains of the three (five) animals, (rocks near the beach), but others live (and swim) now in the sea.[24]

A7. *Inuri : the origin of natural phenomena*

Inuri (a big snake) lived on (the island of) Rumberpon. There were (also) three sisters. Inuri proposed to the eldest one, wanting to marry her, but she refused saying : "Who likes to marry a snake? I want to marry human males, don't I? I am afraid of this snake". Inuri made the same request to the second eldest, but she too did not like it, and said the same words as her sister : "Who wants to marry this snake, I hate him".

Inuri then proposed to the youngest of the girls and she agreed, saying : "This snake, let me merely marry him. Were he a lizard, I would only marry him, were he a dog I would merely marry him, were he a mouse I would just marry him". She blamed her two sisters : "This snake, the two of you are afraid of him, but I merely marry him".

Inuri really married her. In the night-time when they slept he changed into a human being. His skin he laid aside. As soon as the daylight came he donned the snake-skin and he became a snake, but during the night he left his (snake-skin) and was a human male.

(At daybreak) his two brothers-in-law paddled to the sea, they took shell-fish. They brought them to the shore and there they roasted their meal. Inuri tasted the shell-fish and they tasted good. Then Inuri said : "These shell-fish are very good indeed. Are there many of them to be found ?" His brothers-in-law said : "There are many. To-morrow morning we (will row our canoe again) take some others". Inuri said : "I will join you and paddle".

Then, the next morning, the three of them paddled to the sea and they made Inury lie in the bow (of the canoe, near the ornamented bow-piece) and coil himself there until the bow-part (of the canoe [sneber]) was filled, laying his head on the edge of the carved bow-piece.

The two brothers-in-law had taken two hatchets, hiding them in the sail. And so the three of them paddled (rowed), and Inuri watching (the sea-bottom) saw a small shell-fish and said : "There is a shell-fish, do we take it ?" The brothers-in-law said : "That one is not big, we go on, let it remain". They paddled further and Inuri saw another small shell-fish and said : "Don't we take that one ?" The brothers-in-law said : "That one is not big, we go on let that one remain".

They paddled further on and then he (Inuri) saw a giant shell-fish (tridacna or chamagigas) and said to his brothers-in-law : "This big one, don't we take him?" The brothers-in-law said : "Yes, that one we'll take". He asked : "In what way do we take that one?" Then the brothers-in-law sent him, saying : "You just dive".

And they instructed him : "Dive to the bottom, bite in the diagonal closing muscle". When Inuri did as he was told : dived and bit into the diagonal closing muscle, the shell pinched the head of Inuri.

Then two brothers-in-law unrolled the sail to get the hatchet, One of them jumped fast to the bow and started to hew Inuri into fillets. One fillet became a surf wave, one fillet became wind, one fillet became rain, one fillet became thunder, one fillet became lightning, one fillet became a spout, one fillet became a crocodile, one fillet became a porpoise.

All of these (new created phenomena and animals) chased the two brothers to the shore. The two of them escaped by fleeing into the interior of the island. The fillet which became a surf-wave shaved the island Jeninbere. That cape is called "Inuri-dis-i" (Inuri shaved her).[25]

Note from the writer : "In 1886 traveling along the Northcape of Jeninbire, my crew, all of them from the island of Roon, told me Inuri himself had grated the rock bare and smooth with his tail, when his head was pinched in the shell".

A8. *Sentani*[26]

Introduction

In primeval times earth and human beings did not yet exist.

There was only darkness, utter darkness.

The only existing object was an egg.

Then the Northern wind blew (from heaven), touched the egg and broke the shell and out of the egg came a female being named Kani (earth).

In the beginning heaven (the sky) hovered over the earth at a very close range. The first human beings could easily climb and descend to and from heaven by way of a huge banyan tree (yowake) with rattan and a rope made of the clouds.

a) *Warowo and Mahowé, fathers of mankind*[27]

Inside the earth lives the spirit (uarofo)[28] named Warowo. He was not alone there, because another uarofo joined him.

On a certain day this uarofo, Mahowe was his name, dug a way upwards to the surface. He used for this job a stone axe which he had made. He reached the surface of the earth just on the island of Ajau. The hole he made is still visible.

Mahowe built for himself a house and made a drum. After having done this he blew on a conch-shell and beat his drum.

A female spirit named Tariaka living in the village of Tabati (on the seashore) heard the blowing and the boom of the drum and decided to have a look. Thus she went (in South-Western direction) and arrived at Ajau. She had brought some presents with her namely a grilled sea-fish, some pork and parcels of sago-porridge.

The parents of Tariaka found their way to Ajau, and they found a dwelling-place on the cape (opposite Ajau, in a place now named Ifar-ketjil (the small[kendin]-Ifar).

After the arrival of the parents, Mahowe gave them a small blue bracelet made of stone as dowry. And that was the way in which Mahowe got Tariaka as his wife.

Mahowe and Tariaka had many children and these children were normal human beings. After the maturity of these children, the two spirits (uarofo) went back inside the earth through the hole Mahowe once dug to get to the surface of the earth.

As a remembrance of their father his sons carved his image out of wood, which they called Mahowe too.

In times of need and stress the names of Mahowe and Tariaka are still mentioned, they are called upon to give help and support.

After Mahowe had withdrawn himself his power was transferred to his eldest son. He became therefore the first Ondoforo over all his brothers and sisters.

This rank was transmitted to the following generations and became the prerogative of the eldest son.

(Quite another version is given by Wirz, 31, 1928. His informants told him a uarofo dug the people out of four different holes : Samforo, Saboiboi, Ifar, Kabiterau-Puyo; these four groups were dug out in that order. The last investigation made by Jac. Hoogerbrugge resulted in, it may be, the complete text, and is therefore very important.)

b) *Mehué, and the first human beings*[29]

Mehue lived inside the earth. When he had enough men and women with him there, he made a drum which he gave the name of Ghawachu (gha : twilight; wachu : drum). He made also two stone axes and a bracelet out of a conch-shell.

By beating his drum Mehué called upon the people to come together, because they wanted to go out of the earth.

One of them of the Monim-clan died. Then they built a dwelling-place to shelter them during the night.

Mehue then ordered his servant (ufoi)[30] upwards. This servant did not come back (so they waited). When he came back at last he brought the good news : there is an island and it is a place good to live in.

The people of Mehué were angry with him because they had to wait so long. So the ufoi started to cry and did not like to join them when they were to go to the surface of the earth.

He said : "I will stay here inside the earth and when you die you will come inside the earth again".

The people buried Monim and Mehué went further.

He reached the surface of the earth on the highest point of the island of Ajau, named Puhikere. The Ondi-(clan) came out on the spot named Navel (Pulende). (Nowadays the church is built on that spot.) Tokodo (clan) came out near the Western end of the island, named Wakaré. Ibo and Monim (clans) broke the surface at Naisow (now called small-Ifar).

After this they started to build houses.

Mehué had no wife so he married a woman out of the East, from Walagham, her name was Jochumòchò. Ondi married Tokodo's daughter, Tokodo married Ondi's daughter.

Mehuwé became Ondoafo and war-leader. He started to make war with the people in the East from Asei-Ayapo. With the Western people he also waged a war and with the Abele men of the South. To assist him in this last war he pleaded for help from the Hokoi-group, which came from Walagham. Hokoi did indeed assist but asked the Ondi-group and the Tokodo what the reason was that they did not take part in the wars of Mehué. They answered : "We are ondoáfo only so we could not take part in a war on our own behalf".

At that time the groups dispersed.

When someone wanted to wage a war, the only possibility was to ask Mehué's permission. Mehue was the big chief (ondoafo-kabam) and he was superior to all other ondoafo's.

In the West another important ondoafo and war-chief lived, named Marwéri. In the East another one named Ohei.

Since Mahué was ondoafo-kabam 17 of his descendants were in power. (This makes 17 generations, all mentioned.) The three outstanding leaders are mentioned here. Namely : Mehué as ' the tree", and three generations, called branches of the original tree, were : Jochu, Palo and Daime. (Their offspring became the original Sentani-people and they have their villages in the central Islands in the midst of the lake.)[31]

c) *The first immigrants* (*the way in heaven*)

The inhabitants of the village Abar on the islet of Aitemare originally dwelled on the coast of the Humboldt bay, at cape Juar (a rocky cape at the "gateway" of Jayapura. They lived near the village Kayu-Batu, one of the few villages whose inhabitants know the art of pottery).

On their cape grew an enormous banyan-tree (yowake) the crown of which reached the vault (arch) of heaven. The village people climbed the yowake until they arrived at the top and in this manner they reached heaven. Being on the heavenly platform they started to walk in the Southerly direction until they reached a spot just above the islet of Aitemaru. They saw just below them the island and it looked very good to them.

They brought with them a long piece of rattan (others said : the air-roots of the banyan-tree were used) and they lowered themselves until the surface of the island was reached.

(Others said : Seeing the great distance between them and the island they became frightened. Therefore they first let down a cooking-pot (made of clay) and after that a dog (jochu) and when this operation appeared to be succesful, they descended too and safely reached the island.)

The first man who put his foot on the island was Pukaro, then all the others followed.

Their first food was earth, (a special kind of edible clay). An old woman from the Humboldt bay taught them how to eat sago and coconuts.

Especially mentioned was the fact that these Abar-people were nearly giants in their appearance. They fought their battles and made raids resulting in robbery everywhere. They even went far into the interior to the South.

Their fame ended with a horrible revenge from the Sentani-people : black magic finished nearly all of them, only a few were left alive.

The same fate was mentioned by other informants. They said : The former village of Nerebu was attacked by the Abar-people, but the Nerebu in retaliation fought bravely. Most of the Abar people found their death, but the same was true of the Nerebu-people. They had to pay with heavy losses and afterwards vanished.

(Thus far the first but not complete version of this legendary myth;) the real background and events are dealt with in our next myth.

d) *The first people in heaven and on earth*[32]

The fist human beings lived in the village Yobuma-Wolo-bangka (yo = village; buma = above, heaven; bangka = empty).

There lived the Warofoboiro (warofo = spirit) together with the Wali-men.

The Wali-men had to work very hard. The chief of all Boirero was a man who was mean and cruel. When the men, after their daily task, came back from the gardens, the food was not fairly shared. The Wali-men only got the bad parts and the women gave the good parcels to their warofo-husbands only.

After this went on during a certain time Wali took the decision to send his servant (ufoi) named Puloliwai to Haboi on the earth to invite him to come upwards.

Haboi came to Yobuma and then Wali proposed to Haboi to kill the chief of the Warofoboiro. That night Haboi remained in the village and slept there.

The day after (that night) all the men went to work in the gardens. When they came back in the evening and the women had prepared the food, all the men came together and surrounded the chief of the Warofo, who was sitting in their midst distributing the food.

Haboi who came also, had brought a dagger named Welodeuw-fi-embai (fi = porridge of sago; embai = one). After a few moments Haboi stabbed the chief and thereafter the other men killed him.

After this had happened Haboi cut the corpse of the chief into pieces and divided them among the Walofoboiro. The Wali-men did not want anything of it.

The corpse of the chief Boirero was distributed among the high mountains, and Haboi said during this act : "Boirero, stay in the mountains according to the order of Wali. When Wali gives the command to kill somebody just obey that order".

Haboi then nominated Waliminsake as the chief of the

group. After having completed this he descended to Yomocho-(village) Now Waliminsake had a younger brother, who every day went hunting with his dog. Every day they caught something. When Waliminsake ordered his brother to stab and to kill his dog, he (the younger brother) refused and they started to quarrel.

When his brother went hunting again, Waliminsake ordered that a long rattan should be cut in the North, but when they let down the rattan (to the earth) apparently it was not long enough. After that they cut a rattan in the South.

(All) the people now came together and they looked downwards. First they threw a mat down (to the earth) and nothing happened to it, it did not go to pieces, the people danced.

Then they lowered a rattang-ring (maoka = ring of plaited rattan to place an earthen-ware cooking-pot with a bulging bottom on) and after that the cooking-pot itself. The cooking-pot remained whole, hence the people danced again.

Now they threw a dog (jochu) and the animal stayed alive. After that the people descended-men and women-along the rattan. Waliminsake went first and when he reached the earth safely, he saw to it that all the people descended safely (to the earth). They reached the earth at Jewaoke (a kind of tree), Jebeui (a cape), and Taime (a tree).

After everybody was safe they walked in the direction of Kolohan, near the present village of Abar. The man Henaro went further to the village of Depapre. The people of Netar, Babrongko en Nelebu (a group now disappeared) walked from Kolohan to look for a canoe, and they met a man from Abar (the events went on and on : each group got to his own place : Nelembu, Adau, Ifar-Baberongko).[33]

c) *Immigrants from the East and the snake*[34]

In the beginning a group of people lived in the East. Their village was named Fenemyo-Wauwauyo high in the mountains. (The place is located behind Omaka east of the border between Irian Jaya and Papua-New Guinea.) Their high chief was Dohayo. On a certain day he planned to nominate all the ondoforo's, and on that occasion they planned to celebrate this nomination.

Everybody went to the forest in order to prepare their adornment. Only a son of the Taime's (mountainpeople) could not get what he wanted, because all the feathers were already used. (His mother then urged him to climb up a banyan tree : "hide there and shoot, but not kill, some birds of paradise." So he did and he got three still living birds. He donned these birds and was admired (because the birds were alive).)

All the people had already come together in order to celebrate the occasion by a dancing-feast.

Suddenly it seemed as if the earth started to shudder, mountains in the vicinity rumbled.

At that very moment a huge snake, Ahakai-Yoblo (or Yabero) came out of the earth. It seemed he was very angry; he crept to the dancing-site and crawled there with his (long) body.

The mother of the ondofolo (was the first one) who saw the snake and called the inhabitants saying : "Here is something as big as a mountain". Hearing her voice the people came out of their houses, they saw the snake and became terribly frightened.

(At once) they started to collect valuables in order to appease the monster with these gifts. But it was not satisfied with these valuables. Therefore the mother of the ondofolo gathered all her valuables and adornments and adorned Taime with them and she decorated him as beautifully as possible. His hair was dyed with red colourstuff (mèlè) and the three living birds of paradise she inserted into his hair. She rubbed his body with coconut-oil (mélé-bu).

After that Taime came from the house and appeared on the site.

Instantly the snake opened his jaws in order to swallow Taime. Then the old men spoke to the snake : "(Better) shut your mouth and straighten your tail, so that Taime is able to sit on it (to ride on your back)".

The snake obeyed and so Taime and the snake left the dancing-site out to the sea. The snake crept into the sea and swam as a ship to the West.

The mother of Taime stood on the beach and looked; she remained there and petrified into a rock. (Nowadays there is still on that spot a coral-reef near the village Vanimo).

The snake continued to swim and where his body twisted bays and capes came into existence.

The snake swam via Skow and Tabati to a place called Nafri (Hebele). There Taime changed his adorments. They went over the hills and arrived at the lake (Sentani) near Umabo-Kaikiri on the shore.

The head of the snake went in the direction of the islet Tasindjau-Yokoba. And after that the snake disappeared under the surface of the water with Taime on his back.

When all these events had happened all the people, gathered on the dance-site, scattered in every direction.

A part of them, the Ohei-group, followed the path the snake had taken. In Skow part of them had to stay behind because they had sore legs. Others went further to Tobati-Nafri and from there to the place called Umabo-Kaikiri at lake Sentani, located in the mountains behind the recent village Asei.

There they had to fight with the tribes living there. When peace was agreed the people of the East could settle on the shores of the lake.

When they arrived in Yomokoyo-Haliauyo, three groups lived there. 1. Yomoko-Powondo; 2. Toasobo-Kamoto; 3. Wali-Nelelo, with his younger brother Abalendo.

Later on the Oheis of Yomokoyo moved to the island, since called Asei-Ohei. From there the family-groups (clans) split up and this was the origin of the villages Ajapo, Yoka, Waena and Asei-ketjil (the small Asei).

The way of the snake Yabero[35] (a variation of e)

Once upon a time the tribe (clan) with their chief (ondoforo) Dohaya lived in the interior, behind Omaka (terr. of New Guinea). It happened once when Dohaya was working in his garden that a very big snake appeared and Dohaya fled. The next morning the snake came into the village and proposed to the ondoforo to join him. The snake Yabero agreed that the ondoforo should ride on the snake's back, and then he crawled in the western direction to Nafri and further on to lake Sentani.

The snake swam on the surface of the lake until his head reached the spot which now is named Ayapo. His tail still pointing to the east the snake disappeared in the depths of the lake, the ondoforo still riding his back. There he must still be present. Every now and then he makes the water of the lake foam which is a bad omen, for it means that soon a member of the ondoforo-clan has to die.

When the Taime (mountain-people) saw their ondoforo disappear, they just followed the still visible trail of the snake. They started as a big group, but later on they split up into three sections : Ohe, Waima and Sobeiburu.

The ondoforo's were in the lead. When it became dark or when the fog covered the beach and hills their leader struck his drum, so everybody knew the right direction.

The Ohe-group arrived at the shore of lake Sentani on a spot now named Yoka, just opposite the village Ayapo.

They started to build some rafts, but they were no good for the purpose. They just sank, petrified and are still South of Yoka near the shore, their name is Hobobwé.

After that they built better ones which served the purpose well, they hoisted sail (of coconut-tree leaves) and arrived in due time at Ayapo and later on at Asé, where the Ohes remained.

(These were all strong and healthy people, the weak and wounded ones were left behind in the village Nafri on the sea-shore.)

Arriving at Ase they elected their ondoforo. The first one had not the capability to arrange the life of the people, so they elected another one. The same situation arose, but then they chose the clan Atasa, and this appeared succesful. He was able to arrange the ceremonials and celebrations, giving the participants their fair share (and the guests likewise).

Thus Atasi (Ohé) remained in power and so did his succesors through many generations.

The 7th ondoforo (of the 7th generation) named Taisa had two sons, Pena and Abuhé. These two men started an argument about some decoration-pattern of one of their canoes.

Abuhe, the youngest of the two did'nt like the fighting and therefore he moved along with the strongest men of his relatives to the East were he built a village, Ayapo. This village was divided into three sections (Yoho) Deda (in the midst), Kau (on the western end), and Mebri (in the eastern section).

(The descendents of the Ohé from Ase and the Dedas from Ayapo called one another elder and younger brother, but there was always a remarkable tension between the two and their people. The eldest claimed prerogatives which he denied to the younger brother's offspring. This even had consequences for the modern football-games. The elder brother's offspring felt it only proper they should become and remain the winners.)

f) *The journey from West to East, and West again*[36]

1. Feleh and Yukumoko (abridged version)

The ancestor of human beings, Feléh, lived in the village Wai-yohana (wai = Western clouds; yoh = village) in the West.

There was no light, the sky hovered over the earth at close range.

Feléh travelled in a canoe to the East, there was light, to the village of Walaghau.

DoFeléh had caught a casuari-bird and made of its hide the skin for two drums (Bulakoi and Dobongkoi).

When they went to the East from the West the drum Bulakoi fell overboard near Skow.

DoFeléh ordered his men to stop and gave the drum the command to come to the surface again. This happened and

Feléh said to the drum : "We go now to the West again, but when in the future somebody of the Feleh-clan falls ill and he is going to die, please come to the surface and let all hear the voice of your skin as strongly as possible." After this had been said the drum sank again into the sea and the crew continued their paddling.[37]

Coming near the village of Tobati the ufoi (servant) was sent first to contact the Ondoafi of Tabati. After some discussion the Feléh-people were allowed to stay in the Bay of Ria (land of the living). There they built their houses and remained.

It was not for long, because a quarrel burst out with the Tabati-people and Feléh decided to leave the scene. The ondowafi (here called Charsori) heard of the plans of Feléh. and by means of black magic killed the son of Feléh. In order to get permission to bury his son Feléh proposed to the charsori Tabati to pay with products from the garden. This was granted and so it is still done. Feléh went to the South, met the people from the centre part of lake Sentani and got there a nice dwelling-place, namely on the Island which he named Ifalo (now named Ifar) meaning : Western-wind, as a memory of the fact that the Western-wind had brought them to the land of light and life.)

2. From earth to heaven and the East (Marwéri)[38]

Marwéri (the man who is wearing a loincloth).

In primeval times heaven hovered over the earth very closely. The people could climb upwards very easily.

Marwéri left the West and took his way to the village in heaven called Yobuma and there he let (his people) cut a tree in order to build a canoe which could take them all.

The tree was cut in the West.This being finished Marweri lifted the sky so that his crew could travel the way to the East.

In the East he met the man Ondikelew who lived in the village of Walaghauyo. Marwéri stayed there for a while and then left for the island of Pononyo-Melanyo. At this spot they built a village and a very big house named Yebeisoro.

When this was ready they found that there was nothing to decorate the house with and therefore Marwéri had to leave his people.[39] He now ordered the clouds to form ropes. These ropes Marwei climbed and he arrived in Yobuma. There he met the old woman Ururu Deiware who was just occupied with the making of an earthenware cooking-pot. Marweri asked her what she was doing and she told him : I am making a terai (earthenware-pot). Then Marwéri asked her whether she would give the pot to him. She was to stow it away until he came back to take the pot with him.

After having said this (words) Marwéri walked the road to the East until he arrived in the village of Star of the East. He did not remain there but went further to the village Morning-star. But Marwéri went further to the East until he came to the house of Ondikelew Sebefoi. There all the children who saw him coming, while they were playing there, called him : "Stranger, stranger, from where are you coming?"

Ondikelew heard the voice of the children, looked and saw Marwéri coming. In former times he had only called the man Marwéri, but now he added Marwéri, who is coming from the North.

The two friends now talked about their problems. Marwéri told about his new house and his lack of decoration-material. It appeared Ondikelew was willing to share his decorations and ornaments with Marwéri. And while the two were discussing these matters thunder and lightning rumbled and shone.

Then Marwéri got the rights of thunder and lightning from Ondikelew, and at once he put the rumbling to a stop.

Marwéri got the secret of the cooking-pot : if he made a black scratch upon the pot, rain would come, and after a white scratch the sun would start to shine.

After these events Marwéri went to the ladder leading to the earth and went back to his new village Pononjo-Melanjo. The ornaments which he brought along were applied inside and on the outside of his house. The power over thunderstorm and lightning and rain was stored away too.

The time that Marwéri had to marry drew near. To arrange a good match Marwéri sent two ufoi, but on the earth they could not find a partner who suited Marwéri well. Therefore the two went to the heaven-village Yobuma and there they met the girl Yasi (morningstar) and she agreed to follow. So did the second girl Kerosai (a star ... ?). The two of them consented and the dowry was paid right away with glass beads. The counter-gift was a pig.

On the day the two girls were ready to descend, old people saw them to the (banyan ?) ladder. There they could see the village of Marwéri and they started to cry because until then nobody went there to marry. They promised Marwéri if he ever ran into trouble with the rain he could trust to their assistance. After this had been said the two girls descended to the earth, Marwéri married the two girls. One of them died soon, but Yasi bore him a son, a snake, and after that two more children, this time two birds.

Troubled about the lack of a real human son, Marwéri sent his wife away. She put the snake in a basket on her head, went to the forest and seeing a huge tree, she worked charms on the banyan so that it became so short that she was able to climb into the top branches, and then by the same means she lifted the banyan up again.

While she dwelled thus in the treetop an eagle came and let himself down next to her saying in a soft voice : "Old woman, old woman, I live here right below your dwelling-place".

The woman said she was hungry, so the eagle flew downwards and took food out of a canoe on the lake. After that she complained because she had no house to live in. Then the bird swooped downwards again and took a small house in his claws from the lake-side.

Shortly after these events the woman gave birth to twins, two (real human beings) and she named them Marwéri and Sio.

(The story went on telling about the discovery of the woman and her two sons. When the father Marwéri was told about his sons he went in search of the two boys. At first his wife kept him at bay by using charms but at last she yielded, and gave her two sons on condition that she could remain. She refused to join the human beings because she was metamorphosed into a wood-spirit. She then renounced her two sons and she remained in the forest with her two bird-children).

When the two sons arrived in the village of Pononjo-Melanjo, Marwéri, their father, died. But before this happened he transferred all his rights and powers to his eldest son.

(And this became the point of departure of a turbulent history.)[40]

A9. *Creation of men and the secret of eternal life on earth*[41]

The first human beings emerged from the mountain Davonsero (Cyclop). They were a brother and sister.

They lived together with their father and when the two reached maturity, they married.

Then the father died but the next day he arose from the dead.

His two children saw him coming and could not believe their eyes, but cried out : Father.

But he was really alive again, hence he must know the secret of eternal life.

Nothwithstanding this fact was true, he could not tell this secret to his children; he tried very hard (but did not succeed because his son and daughter did not understand the language of the secret).

The father then tried to share the secret with the animals : snakes, spiders and all animals which are now able to cast off their old skin. And this time he succeeded, but during this transfer of the secret, the father himself lost it.

Hence he had to die again and so after some time he did. The secret of eternal life on earth went with him into the grave.

As a symbol of this eternal life there only remain the animals and living beings which are able to cast their old skin and become every time new-born again.

These living beings are also the symbol for the state of bliss, (the Utopia in the future).

A10. *The woman of the east and the snake of heaven*[42]

The woman Ajechoi in the East drifted off to the sea, floating on some driftwood. Month after month went by and the driftwood with the woman floated on the currents of the ocean in Westerly direction.

She came near the coast still clinging to the driftwood, which drifted near the surf (which was pounding the beach).

The surf caught the driftwood and washed wood and woman ashore. The woman landed near the burned rocks south of the present village Ormu.

Ajechoi climbed onto the beach by scrambling up the slope of the rocks (in order to be safe from the battering surf).

From there she moved on in search of a place to live in. She found, after some time, a cave in which she remained for the time being.

She sat (at the entrance) of the cave and thought about her land and relatives. How far away seemed her land of origin and her heart became filled with sadness which she uttered in a bitter complaint. She mentioned in her song of sorrow, she had nothing, no food, no adornments according to her rank.

This song-of-sorrow was heard by Maiwa, the snake of heaven and he descended and kept her company.

He consoled the woman, called forth every kind of food and adornments and remained with her in the cave.

This resulted in marrying and the couple dwelled henceforth together.

When after a while the woman appeared to be pregnant her snake-husband left her and went to his abode in the sky. His wife he left behind. When her belly became very big, she knew the time to bear was drawing near. But she could not bring forth children, because she always remembered her relatives (and the elderly women who assist wives in labour).

But, when her time was really due, her snake-husband came back again. He caressed her and her womb opened and the fluid came out. Hence she started to bear.

First she gave birth to a lot of grass, then a snake named Mugu, and in quick succession every kind of small and big animals. After this had happened the father-snake put a stop to the bearing of his wife and gave some advice to the animals just born. He ordered them : "All of you go and hide yourself in the forest, the dust of the soil will be your food. Take cover under the trees".

To the snake(s) he said : "Don't bite human beings who call you brother, because then you have nothing to fear. But, if they say nothing at all they have to die (then you are allowed to bite)".

After having arranged all this he went back to his wife and then she continued to bear again. This time she brought forth four humans beings, two pairs of twins.

Two of them were girls and the other two were boys.

The boys got the name Awi and Nafri, the names of the girls are a secret (but both are named Baäl).

When the four human beings grew to maturity, they had no mates who matched them (because there were no other human beings). So the two brothers Awi and Nafri took their sisters in marriage. The offspring of these two couples were many, and these intermarried again. In the course of time a multitude of people came into existence and they had no room for them all in their place of origin.

That was the reason why they dispersed to the East, others to the West and many scattered in Northern direction (on the islands).

In reality there were originally three sons, the third one had the name of Ononai.

(This was the beginning of mankind all the animals.)

Here the narrative ends.

SECTION B

THE SUN AND THE MOON[43]

B1. *The origin of sun and moon in Sentani*[44]

The ancestor Haboi had his abode in the village Yomoko. It was dark and the sky was black and (seemed) closed. Therefore they (the inhabitants of the village) decided to lift the heaven a little bit and to lower the earth, in order to have light. This accomplished, they saw the people had no fire and no water. (Cf. the origin of water and fire in a later section.)

When the people still dwelled in the village of Yomoko, men went hunting and fishing, while the womenfolk were in the village. They were knitting fishing-nets.

Close to the village a spirit (uarofo) lived in a huge tree. This uarofo came in the midst of the day and seduced women. Only the wife of Haboi he left alone.

The women told nothing to their husbands, they kept it secret. Until on a certain day the men really saw the uarofo. Hence the men called Haboi and Wali (and told them whom they had seen).

Haboi then interrogated the women, his own wife too. She answered : "Indeed even Wali's wife has done it, but I did'not do likewise", Haboi (after having heard all these witnesses) ordered to collect much firewood and to pile it up around the tree in which the uarofo stayed. He intended to burn the spirit in that way.

The next day nobody went into the woods, everybody wanted to assist in burning the spirit. Everyone had brought spears, bows and arrows to kill him.

About noon, when the fire started to be hot, the spirit handed his children (there were five of them) and his wives (to the people surrounding the tree).

The people received them, but did no harm to them because they wanted the spirit.

When the fire became hotter, the spirit extended his right hand out of the tree and handed down his carrying-bag. First a bag of a plain colour, which Haboi took and laid near him on the ground. After this the spirit gave a bag with one stripe which Haboi laid on the ground too. After this one the spirit handed down bags with two, three, four etc. until at last the bag having twelve stripes appeared.

In the same way it happened once more with the loin-cloths. Only the one having twelve stripes as decoration Haboi accepted and he slung this one (around his waist).

Now the spirit himself appeared and tried to escape. Haboi however speared him in his left eye. Then the spirit asked : Who has thrust me?" Haboi answered : "I did". Then the spirit spoke the following prophecy : "The wife of Haboi will bear children, but the eldest one I shall always kill. Therefore the youngest one shall have to succeed him". Having said these words the spirit dived into the water. But another man speared him again. The ghost (emerged) and asked : "Who was the one who thrust me?" "I did" Heungka from Wali answered. The spirit predicted : "The spear you used to thrust me, I shall take with me to the North and I shall spear in the Southern direction to the offspring (descendants) of Heungka, whoever he may be".

After (having said these words) the uarofo vanished in the water and he emerged in the East.

He summoned Haboi, and asked : "Where am I?"

Then Haboi said to the uarofo : "You have become the

sun, and your left eye, which I speared out of its socket, became the moon". First he went from North to the South, but shortly thereafter he descended and it became dark. The second time from South to the North, the third time from the West to the East, but every time it became (very soon) dark. The fourth time he arose in the East and set in the West. Until now this happens ever since.

After this was settled Haboi shared the loin-cloths and the bags whereupon the men scattered (dispersed).

One group went to Yakonde, one of them to Doyo, one to Aséi, one to Ayapo, one to Poeë, and the last one to Demta (on the sea-shore).

And this is the reason why descendants of Wali are dwelling in all these places.

B2. *The moon, embarrassment and surprise in Yafi*[45]

Long ago there lived on the mountain Tiwar, in the eastern section of the Yafi-area a man named Sangrar.[46]

During the day he was an ordinary human being, but at night he became very tall (like a giant). He roamed the country between the Tiwar mountains in the East and the Riwi or Tar in the West. Sangrar did not have a house, most of the time he stayed in the Riwi, and according to tradition that is the place he still remains. From Riwi-mountain he was able to have a perfect view over all the surrounding land, and there was "light".

During the nights Sangrar applied his secret power in order to give (an appropriate) shape to the earth and landscapes. He lifted the mountains or lowered them. He dug the course of the rivers, planted complete forests etc. For example : He lifted the Riwi-mountain, created the hill, nowadays the location of the Sungwer village. Sometimes he dropped pieces of mountains, of which you can see clearly the remains, e.g. the Komdrok-hill.

In the neighbourhood of the recent village of Ibela some people built a hamlet consisting of only one, but a very long house. This hamlet was named Nuweo and there dwelled remarkable people. Each couple, husband and wife, had grown into bisexual beings. Their backs had grown attached to each other.

This condition made work in the gardens very wearisome and hard. Nevertheless they had grown different kinds of tuberous plants and vegetables such as "candle".

These plants grew exuberantly, but very soon it was discovered some stealing was going on : the proceeds of the candle-vegetable had disappeared.

In order to detect the thief a small boy remained in the garden, hidden between the sugarcane.

This boy saw a bright unknown being (the moon) emerge out of a certain tree. He stole the vegetables and having done this he disappeared into the hole of the tree.

Towards daylight the boy ran home and told everything he had seen. Immediately all the people went to the tree concerned, hewed at its base until it fell and then started to hew the trunk into pieces. Every time they nearly reached the moon he withdrew further into the tree. In the last piece however he was caught and put into a carrying-net. This net disrupted through the heavy weight of the moon, so the men took several nets and caught the moon in that way.

Wrapped up this way they brought the whole parcel home and hung it on the ceiling beams. They saw that some kind of liquid was pressed out of the moon-body, it seemed to be a kind of fat dripping from the moon-parcel. People tried cooking and roasting their food with this grease, and it tasted just fine.

On a certain day everybody left home, except two small children, to hunt and collect vegetables. Before the people left home, they had shut the house as well as possible and forbidden the children to let anyone enter.

But nevertheless just on that day the famous Sangrar paid a visit to the hamlet. He knocked at the door, asking for some fire.

The children gave him the fire through an opening in the wall of the house, saying they were not allowed to let anybody in.

Sangrar however threatened them saying he would do them much harm if they would not let him come in.

The frightened children then opened the door.

Inside the house Sangrar asked for some baked sago and as it tasted extraordinarily good, he finished all he got hold of.

The children told him the good taste of the sago was due to the fact that it was mixed with fat dripping from the moon.

Hearing this Sangrar wanted (at once) to see the moon. He opened the carryall-bags but the moon slipped through and dropped into a water-reservoir. With his filthy and stained hands Sangrar tried to get hold of the moon, but the greasy and slippery moon-body just dropped back every time, so at last he was marked with many dirty black spots.

The moon, embarrassed by this treatment, got bored and started to climb one of the poles of the house and rested for a while on the top of the roof. Sangrar did not quit his endeavour and tried to get hold of the moon. Even when the moon went upwards in the air Sangrar made a kind of ladder which he climbed in order to reach and catch the moon. He nearly succeeded, but then the moon took hold of Sangrar's hair, ascending as high as he could.

He took Sangrar with him, asked him the names of several villages, and Sangrar told him the names. This lasted until they came to an area unknown to Sangrar and it was here that the moon turned Sangrar's body, still hanging from his hair, and dropped him into the top of a coconut-tree. The young sprouts of the tree pierced the bottom of Sangrar and much blood dripped from his big wounds.

People who were passing by saw the blood and freed him from his dangerous position.

Sangrar, thankful for the assistance he got, split the bi-sexual human beings into couples an taught them later on how to copulate and to multiply.

B3. *Whence the moon and the stars came according to the Wombe-people*[47]

In primeval times a man named Kungu lived South of the recent village of Mòlo-òf at a place named Wombé.[48]

He was in the possession of the moon, which he had stored away in a big sago-tray. The moon was so hot that Kungu was enabled to cook his meals on it.

On a certain day Kungu went to the small Sangur-lake to prepare sago-flour (by splitting a sago-tree, pounding the content into pulp and rinsing-out the starch.)

At that place Kungu met two women, they were sisters and Kungu took the two of them as his wives to Wombe...

... The two wives had to work very hard at Kungu's demand and they did not like it at all. So they decided to take revenge by sewing up their private parts in order to prevent Kungu from having intercourse with them. Kungu discovered what the two had done and attached in two different trees a small and very sharp stone axe.

After that he ordered the two women to get him some "ján" (red-fruits) and pinang, so they had to climb just those two trees in which Kungu had attached the axes. In this way the axes cut open again what they had sewn up and so their revenge came to nought.

The two wives now furiously angry tried to poison their husband by mixing poison in his sago-porridge. But Kungu coming home from his work tasted the food and discovered what his two wives had in mind and therefore he refused to eat his meal. On a certain day Kungu's brother-in-law came to visit him. His wives were not at home and so Kungu welcomed this relative in the most friendly manner.

The custom of the moon was to appear out of his sago-tray about the evening-time, the time when the sun sets. It was namely his task to illuminate the house. But the visitor did not know anything about this (regular happening).

Kungu had left his house and his visitor saying he wanted, if possible, to shoot a pig in his sago-garden.

About sunset he had not yet returned when suddenly, about the usual time, the moon emerged illuminating the house (as bright as daylight).

The brother-in-law, frightened by this sight, started in his terror to strike the moon with a stick (hence the many stains the moon now has) and it broke into two halves.

One of the halves, still intact, fled as moon upwards to the sky, the other half struck into splinters followed suit, and these small pieces became the stars.

Kungu coming home saw what had happened. However, he kept his temper and did not take revenge at once. He could wait (cf. the great floods II). After some time he got a son Kelébi and a daughter named Noad.

B4. *The narrative of the maiden, the moon and the sun*[49]

In primeval times there was, in the village Tarau (on the island of Japen, Geelvinkbay) a maiden who got the moon-sickness (menstruation). She had already reached her marriageable age, but to marry appeared to be impossible, because she (never) recovered from her illness.

She was confined to her sleeping-mat and place, which always became dirty[50] by her sickness.

She gave offence and her relatives (parents and the like) were shocked by it. They started to talk about her condition, they called her names, mocked and even scolded and insulted her all the time.

Therefore she ran away to another house where the inhabiants were also related to her. But after some time (what happened at home) now this was repeated all over again. People started talking about her. Also they were tired as they always had to change the boards of the floor dirtied by the maiden's flow (everything became stained by the sickness of the girl).

On a certain day whilst all her relatives were going into the sago-wood to prepare sago-flour, she called a sparrow bird. She said : "(Please) fly my message (wijakipin) to the honoured sun (sang ori[51]) i.c. On earth lives a female named Dang Paik (the honoured Lady Moon) and she urgently wants your highness to consider a meeting between the two of you. She wants to know if you would agree with the following arrangement. The sun, your highness, will shine in the daytime, but the Lady Moon during the nights".

"If his highness receives my proposal in a good spirit ask him to lower the sky, bring his answer back to me, and I will ascend".

Having said all these words to the sparrow (who flew to the sun) she started to climb a very tall pinang-tree. Then the lady moon lengthened the pinang-tree by means of a long bamboo-stem.

Now the sun lowered the sky unto Lady Moon. When the two of them met, the sky was lifted up again to her (proper) place.

When (sun and moon) the two of them met, Sang Ori said to Lady Moon : "Let it be just as you proposed : you are allowed to shine your light during the nights, and I will shine in the daytime".

In the evening the relatives of the maiden came home from their work in the sago-woods. They did not see the maiden, so they searched everywhere, but could not find her.

But what happened during the night-time? Their house became dark inside, but what kind of light shone outside? Whence came this radiating light? From the sky! "Yes there she is, the one whom we despised and hated. It is a great, yes a great pity".

People looked upwards to the sky, cried and deplored their behaviour towards the maiden, until this world will end.

B5. *The children of the sun*[52]

The far East of Irian Jaya is named Sup Tabi, (Land of the Sun)[53] by the inhabitants of the Geelvinkbay. This is done because the remarkable myth of the origin of the people of the Humboldt bay was known even by the "strangers" from the Geelvinkbay, who paid visits every now and then. The myth runs as follows :

The primeval God Tab (the sun) fostered for a long time the wish to create human beings on earth. After he had contemplated this (difficult question) a long time he descended to the earth. (Another version says : He sent his brother Yatji.)

First he tried to make a human being out of clay, but he failed with clay from the upper layer. Clay of a deeper layer did not give good results either.

Then Tab started to take blood-red coloured clay from the third layer and this time he succeeded.

But the whole structure was only a shape. This form he had made had hands and legs, but not yet a nose, mouth, eyes, breath nor bones.

Tab now made all these lacking members and organs out of different ingredients, such as : soft wood, the skeleton of a snake and the eyes of the primeval forest-cat.

This accomplished, Tab spoke to this (structure) : "Child, your name is Iria, answer me". And Iria said : "Yes, Father".

Iria then got the instruction from Tab, to walk to the mountain Mér over the plain of Yotefa. He had to come back when Tab should order him to walk home again.

And it happened just that way.

Iria's wife was made out of the rib of Iria and the two of them lived together on the mountain Mér. Their first child was named Dohor, the second one Meach, both of them boys.

After this birth there came sixteen girls, to them no names were given, because they died soon after their birth.

As spirits they are now playing an important role as fate-sisters. They give good and evil omens : Dark clouds arising from the rocky cape Suaja and drifting in the direction of Tabati village indicate a patient will have to die[54].

The spirits of the sisters have their abode on Cape Suaja (behind the village of Kayu-Batu near the entrance of the Humboldtbay.

(In the version just given the birth of the first woman reminds us of the story of Eva, but there is also another version told to the present writer and to Galis too.)

"The deity Tab gave the first man the name Numaditj or Iria (house, place of life) and this first man got two women as his wives out of heaven. After the two got their children, they went back to their place of origin. (K. W. Galis, 1955, 247.)[55]

B6. *Whence came the moon? Origin and treasure producer*

According to our ancestors the moon is a kind of goddess, who gave to human beings much pleasure and wealth in primeval times.

About the origin and the events which took place at that time our ancestors accounted for it in the following narrative :

On a certain day an old woman went to the sea-shore with the purpose to do some rod-fishing.

But, alas, from dawn till the evening not a single fish was she able to catch. With a sore heart and disappointed she went home. The next day, as soon as dawn permitted her (to see anything) she went again, but until nightfall she got no results either. Home she went and there was sadness in her heart.

And so it went on, day after day, all her labour came to nought.

(Therefore she stayed home for a couple of days.)

Then it happened on a certain day when she went again with her fishing-rod, she waited all day until the night fell. And just then (when the sun had already set) she felt her fishing-line was pulled at very strongly : this meant a big fish (at last had nibbled at her bait).

With strong hands and a heart leaping with joy she started with all her strength to pull the big fish to the beach.

Having pulled the fish near to the shore, she saw that her fish was shining brightly while still under (the water-surface).

Utterly amazed in her heart she inspected her big "fish" which was globular and had neither eyes, scales, tail, gills, mouth nor anything else (a fish usually has).

"Karwaro-o" (Spirits of the dead). "Good gracious! What a weird kind of fish is this" she thought to herself, "much better throw it away, this is not a fish at all".

But suddenly the thought arose in her mind : "It is much better if I take home this object and show it to my fellow-villagers". At that time it was night already.

The "object" she had obtained she brought home and stored it away in her bed-room.

Good gracious (Karwar kakuje[57]), how bright was her light in the room and how rich the old woman became.

She considered once more her situation and decided not to let anybody in her village see the weird object. But it happened one day that the old woman left her house having in mind to go once more to the seashore rod-fishing.

Her real aim was to get hold of another "object" like she obtained the first time.

She did not gain what she expected, on the contrary, it soon became clear she would suffer a great loss.

The moment she left home and headed for the beach, some children from the village came to the house of the old woman. They entered her house, discovered the "weird object" and started to play with the shining thing in the bed-room of the woman.

The "object" (could not stand it) and started to roll all by herself out of the room and the house of the woman.

After that she rose slowly upwards from the earth, floating to the sky where she became the moon.

When she was far away already, all the wealth and pleasure and joy of the old woman disappeared and faded away out of her sight.

In these circumstances the old woman became very sad, she nearly died of sorrow.

When she saw (after all these events took place) the bright moon time and again her heart nearly melted : destroyed was her happiness when she considered her fate.

And looking at the full moon, old people remember the wonderfull possibilities, once within reach, and now lost forever.

(The informer closed his narrative with the following remarks : "Greed destroys what mankind once had, greed will make what we possess fade away".

Note. "Greed" as characterizing the events just described, does not cover the real background. What was going on was : the old woman betrayed the most important and basic behaviour principle i.e. cooperation and the sharing of wealth, the sharing of her secret she initially planned to accomplish.

Accumulated wealth means "dead-weight" and is useless. Only circulating goods result in life-giving stimuli in the social-ceonomic process of exchange in a well integrated society.

B7. *People who wanted to gain the moon*[59]

In primeval times there was, on the top of the mountain Inggoro, a village. This mountain was one of the chain of mountains named Inggoirosa (mountain god Inggoiro). Inggoirosa was the highest peak between the villages Paradoi and Wareni. A river, the Ronggaiwa, has its sources (at the slopes of the mountain). In former times our ancestors lived in the mountains, in the (rain) forest and also on the banks of the rivers.

There was found a place where a very big kind of bamboo grew.

People got their subsistence by gardening, hunting and by preparing sago.

As the said people lived on the mountain peak, their enemies could be held at bay in an easy way. (They could cope with every attack), because it is clear our ancestors were accustomed to wage wars continuously.

On the mountain-top however they could live in peace and security and the population was able to increase in great numbers.

Only one thing bothered their children. At the time of full-moon this heavenly body arose out of the valley of Inggoirosa, and looking to the East it seemed the moon must be very near the inhabitants of the mountain-village.

That was the reason why the children wanted to reach the moon. Every day, time and again they cried, they wept in order to get that moon. Even they refused to eat and no suggestion (however kindly proposed to them) could appease them.

And this was the real reason why the people started to consider the (possibility) to build a tower. They discussed the situation and after long deliberations until they all agreed, the descision was taken to build a tower.

As soon the agreement was a fact. everybody started to work. They cut bamboo in great numbers (and the biggest and tallest they could get) and piled them all up on the mountaintop. Everybody, grown-ups and children big and small cooperated. Day after day, month after month they continued their work.

The people who took part were divided into two groups. One group gathered the bamboo material and the other one started to erect and connect (the long bamboo-stems). They did not tire in working every day (in order to complete their job).

The result was they made a kind of big ladder (or huge structure) in the direction of the moon.

At last they neared their goal : the moon was within reach. But, nearly having reached their (ultimate) goal, the moon (came into action) showered a rain of stones onto the structure (now crowded with people).

The huge structure (ladder) collapsed and came tumbling down to the earth.

Among those (people) who fell into the sea, some metamorphosed into dugongs (sea-cows), dolphins, turtle etc.

Those who fell on the land metamorphosed into kangaroos, swine, snakes, mice, tree-kangaroos etc.

According to the belief of the people who came originally from the mountain Inggoirosa it is strongly forbidden (taboo, for) to them to eat the fishes and animals just mentioned.

They say : "Whoever does eat them will become insane, or fall terribly ill, he may even die".

To the descendants of the ancestors, mentioned who do not believe what is said (about this taboo) old (villagers) will say : "Just try to examine the dugongs, they have a beard and they weep (their tears) just like human beings. And have a good look at the kangaroos, the small ones in the trees, they have hands like we have".

All this had happened and therefore very many of our people abstain from eating the animals and fishes mentioned. According to the tradition the present clans Watofa (Watopa) and others are dwelling nowadays in the villages Paradoi and Wareni.

It is told however that even the clans around the Jotefa-bay (near Jayapura, former : Hollandia) originally came into being through the event of the moon-tower. So their original village was Inggoirosa too.

The evidence of this statement is substantiated by the fact, that some Jotefa-clans keep the same taboo rules concerning the sea-mammals mentioned.[60]

This was the story concerning people who tried to gain the moon. About the remains of these events it can be said : The mountains, rivers, the villages are still there. Even the bamboo on the peak of mount Inggoirosa can still be found, however not in such an amount as it apparently used to be in times long ago.

B8. *The children of the moon*[61]

Background

In times immemorial the sun and the moon were on this earth. The sun was the husband and the moon his wife (or : they were two brothers, the elder the sun, the younger the moon).

In the midst of the earth stood a huge banyan-tree and at the time the sun became very bright, human beings dwelled in the shadow of the tree. They found a shelter against the heat of the sun.

In daytime the sun went over the earth from east to west. During the nights the moon gave her light and the people loved it. They went out of their houses and enjoyed her light.

All went well and the people were on their way to multiply and became prosperous, because the earth brought forth her fruits, the women got children and the tree of life, the banyan, gave wealth of every kind that the people needed.

Because the people loved the moon more than the sun, who made them afraid, the sun became angry and when in the night-time he took his way through the underworld the dwarfs inside the bowels of the earth had to convince the sun to rise again in the morning. In order that he should undertake his daily journey, every night the dwarfs reminded him and helped him to conquer the powers of the underworld. They turned a rod and dragged him along. Sometimes we see the blood-stains of the fight against the evil night and underworld-powers in the morning-sky.

The moon was the mother (or the brother) of mankind. Everything went alright in that era. Human beings just imitated the moon and sorrow and death was unknown. No division between life and death, no trouble in daytime or during the nights, but out of the bowels of the earth night and terror threatened.

The dividing of day and night, the tasks of the sun and the moon were the beginning of the dichotomy (meaning culture, struggle, labour over against the time of bliss and abundancy.)

Text

"The belief of all of the Swandibu (beach inhabitants of the East coast of the Bird's Head peninsula) was shown each time the moon started her new course, Then they loved whole-heartedly (the time forever gone) and they cried and wept too.

The reason (of this attitude) is the following :

According to the tale about the "first time" told by our ancestors to us, their sons and daughters, it was said : There was (once upon a time) a quarrel between two beings.

One of the two was an evil spirit (manwén) the other was a real man.

Because all the people liked to listen to the real human being, the evil spirit (manwén) became angry (jealous).

The manwén then cheated the people by hiding himself behind the shrubs and calling (imitating the voice of the real man) the people. A man (hearing the voice) thought it was the good human being's voice and he answered (and he went thither). Then the manwen killed the man.

(After this had happened) the human beings die, but they are not able to arise from death anymore.

If they die they just remain dead.

If the people had been listening to the real human man only, then we should nevertheless have died, after being killed by a manwen, but we would be enabled to arise very soon again. We then should be able to follow the example of the moon : she dies indeed, but after a few days she starts a new life again.

And therefore nowadays when somebody has died in his clan, a son or wife (husband) or father, may be his mother, and this has recently happened, it may be ten days ago and then he sees the moon at that moment he will cry very much.

This habit still exists among elder people, but the younger ones do not know all this anymore.

But (everybody knows) if the moon shines bright, death too is on his way, because the manwens are on their "warpath". Therefore during full-moon-time the moon gives fish, swine in great numbers, but also deaths. There are always many at such a time.

This is the real belief of the Swandirbu people, but this belief too shows many variations.

SECTION C

THE ACHIEVEMENT AND DISCOVERY OF FIRE[62]

C1. *The goddess of fire*[63]

The Sentani-people with their two outstanding leaders Haboi and Wali, lived in the first human settlement the village of Yomoko. They still lived without knowing how to make fire and the use of it. (But this matter was discussed : somewhere fire must exist.)

This was the reason all the people collected their valuables in order to buy the rights to possess the fire.

Wali was the one who started the trip (in search of the fire) and he was way ahead when Haboi visited Wali's place in order to join him. But then Haboi made use of his witchcraft[64] causing Wali much trouble on his journey and so Haboi could overtake him easily. After they met they continued their search together. First they mounted the hill of Handaholo, behind the (recent) village of Yakonde.

There they searched for two days but found nothing. They slept in the wood.

The next morning they suddenly saw smoke ascending from somewhere out of the middle of a big forest. They went to have a look and they walked together.

Arriving at the place (whence the smoke ascended) they saw a woman, but her whole body was ablaze.

The name of the woman was Hokaimiè (i = fire; miè = woman).

Haboi then said to his younger brother he should go to the (fire) woman and ask for some fire. (Wali then went) and the woman gave a flaming piece of wood (a small branch) to Wali. (After they got what they wanted, they started going back to their village.) Wali carried the burning branch.

But when they passed by some water Wali extinguished the fire by dipping the burning branch into the water. He had in mind to go back to the fire-woman once more, because he wanted to possess her.

When Wali went back to the woman, Hokaimiè saw him coming and said : "The fire I gave you could never 'die' (by itself), but I know (what you have in mind) you want to own me by yourself alone, but I warn you".

Wali nevertheless carried on according to his desire, and the woman did not resist.[65] But Wali embracing her was enveloped by the fire and was burned completely.

Haboi waited and waited, but Wali did not come back. At last he decided to ask the woman herself about the whereabouts of Wali. She answered Wali was already dead. Haboi saw the scorched bones of Wali, gathered and bound them together.

After that Haboi in his turn asked the fire-uarofo for some fire. Hokaimiè gave him a burning piece of wood and promised that this fire would not "die" (be extinguished) evermore.

And the same promise would be true for all his descendants too. She added : "If other villages become angry with you, because you have called upon me (to give you the fire), then I will come and destroy all those villages by fire".

The scorched bones of Wali Haboi distributed alike over all the high mountain-summits and scattered them over all (the surrounding hills) also, as a witness of the fire.

After all these events took place Haboi appointed a new chief.

Until now the hills around the lake Sentani are scattered

with black rocks (blackened and scorched by the regular fires by hunting-parties to trap the animals which are shot at when they try to escape the fire). The Sentani people regards these rocks (and tell visitors so) as the petrified remnants of the bones of Wali, but according to the belief of the Sentani-people the black stones are in point of fact the dwelling-places of the fire-ghost (uarofo-i).

(In the belief-system of the Sentani-people however all mountain- and hilltops are potential seats of irrational supernatural powers and ghosts).

C2. *The tale about fire on the island of Padaido*[66]

According to the myth from the island of Padaido near Biak our ancestors, inhabitants of the island, (at that primeval time) were ignorant of the existence of fire.

The food they consumed was merely dried in the heat of the sunshine. They let it dry until the foodstuff became really sun-dried and hard. This sun-dried food was named "ripe" (mjas-mbrai).And after that they just ate their food (every day) sun-dried.[67]

The harvest of their gardens, and fishes caught they flattened and bound them between strips of split bamboo and in this way they just laid this foodstuff in the sun-shine.

Notwithstanding the fact that many tribes and villages knew already the use of fire, warfare hampered contact (between the different islands and areas).

There were wars (and feuds) going on between clans, villages and islands. Therefore it was not safe to travel around and make contacts with each other. In short : contact in a more friendly way was nearly impossible and communication (and sharing of culture) too. Far-reaching and long-lasting voyages were therefore impossible.

And so it was with the villages of the Island of Padaido, the villagers never left their island and village to make long trips and they did not get the knowledge about the making of fire.

On a certain day it happened that two brothers went fishing by means of a net. This net was made from the aerialroots of the pandanus tree.

The fishing of the two brothers was successful and therefore they went to their garden carrying their haul.

In the garden they prepared the fish, and bound them between bamboo-strips; then they placed the pieces on a log in the sun-shine, in order to "ripen" in the usual manner.

Furthermore they pulled some tubers farkia (keladi = colocasia antiquorem) wanting to let them become sun-dried, in order to eat them along with the fishes.

As the two men were waiting, having in mind to let (their food) become sun-dried as usual, their dog suddenly started to bark fiercely at (something) while he was standing near the trunk of a huge banyan-tree (just) outside the garden.

The elder of the two brothers ordered his younger brother to have a look, what could be the reason (of the dog's behaviour). But the younger brother "just pushed back" this command, refusing to accomplish what his brother ordered him to do, saying : "On the contrary, you as the elder and not I, have to go and have a look (investigate)".

Apparently the two brothers were frightened, therefore this reciprocal refusal and the mutual appointing of the task of investigation, which neither of them wanted.

Thus (therefore) the elder of the two (knowing his duty) summoned up courage and off he went to investigate what was going on at the banyan-tree.

While he walked in the direction of the noise from the

barking dog, he raised his face and beheld a goddess of extra-ordinary beauty while her body and breasts were decorated with the most wonderful adornments in great variety.

What his eyes saw was of a terrifying appearence and frightened he wanted to run away. But (before he could run) a very sweet voice sounded from below the banyan-tree saying : "Hi, do not be afraid, because I came from heaven (having in mind) to help you. I remained in my house in heaven, but I saw how poor and miserable your life (on earth) really was all those years, all those days and because I love you and therefore I (descended and) came to assist you".

Having said these words she ordered the two brothers to collect fire-wood as much as possible, and she herself started to make two pieces of tools which would enable her to show how to make fire.

These tools were the fire-drill (aswir) and a piece of soft wood in order to drill holes in it. (While drilling this fire-drill in the soft-wood small holes were made by the end of the drill, and the scrapings made by drilling were heated and eventually caught fire. These smouldering scrapings became the base and material to inflame small branches and dry leaves.)

After the heavenly being had shown the way of getting fire, she asked for some foodstuff. She got fishes and some tubers and roasted them.

The two brothers were afraid to eat this food prepared by fire, so they called their dog and gave some to him first.

When the dog ate in the manner dogs do : swallowing what they like in great quantities, and after a while he did not die, then the two brothers took the roasted tubers and fishes and they liked the taste of it.

Going home after this experience they told and showed everything they just went through.

From that time on, the people of Padaido used the fire and spread the knowledge of the making of it to all their kinfolk.

The second remarkable deed accomplished by the goddess of heaven was concerning the birth of children.

To be exact : our people in those primeval times did not yet know how the birth of a child in a natural way should take place. According to the tales told by our ancestors the Padaido-island people arranged the "birth" of a baby in the following manner.

When the time to give birth to a child drew near the pregnant woman was brought to an old man, who knew the way in which the child could be born.

This was a very old man who dwelled all on his own in a kind of cabin far away from the houses of the village-people.

The site on which he lived was named Njanpraina (nowadays this area is made into a coconut garden by the two clans (kerets) Rumah Ropen and Jarangga, both originally coming from the island of Biak.)

The manner in which the old man brought the child out of the womb of its mother was by way of cutting with a knife.

The old man owned a very sharp knife sharpened on either side and sparkling. When the sun was shining and its rays hit the knife it reflected in a frightening way.

With this knife the old man just split up the abdomen of the woman whose time drew near, and thus he was able to take the child out of the womb.

The child he laid in a wooden bowl filled with (warm) water. But the young mother only could say "good-bye, live long and happy" to her new-born child and then she had to die.

This was the task of the old man and they called him therefore : Mansanak (the splitter).

When the goddess heard about the sad tale concerning the coming into the world of the new-born children, she lingered on for a while.

When for one of the Padaido-women the time to give birth drew near, the goddess started to make clear that there was a natural way to come into the world, Further : she wanted to demonstrate what she said on the woman for whom her people were on the verge of warning the old man.

People believed her words and she said : "We will just sit and wait", and so they did.

Then the time drew very near, but the child came into the world through the narrow canal and ... the mother stayed alive.

After this had happened, nobody ever went anymore to the old man Mansanak.

The people of Padaido however started to sing their mourning song (kajob) about all the young mothers who had lost their lives unnecessarily.

C3. *The noble-woman from the sky* (*Inseren-nankri*)[68 69]

Variant, second version

(The first part of the myth gave the same situationing sketch : The Island of Padaido, no fire, food sun-dried. Two brothers went to their garden, peeled the tubers etc.)

"A woman named Inserennankri (noble-woman of the sky), who had fallen from the sky had landed in the top of the huge banyan-tree, named Ineki-i[70]. (The woman climbed it.) (The tree is still there.) She descended from the tree and saw the two brothers working in their garden. They had no fire, so they prepared the tubers, they pulled out of the soil.

Because they had no fire the princess from the sky summoned the two brothers : "Come hither, I will instruct you how to make fire". She ordered them first to collect some wood from the marpjan-tree[71].

Then she made the tools to make fire (the fire-drill) but when the dry-wood was aflame, the brothers became frightened.

But the sky-woman went on and prepared a meal, she cooked some tubers. The two man were afraid to eat this new foodstuff, so they gave a piece to their dog, and he stayed alive, then the older brother gave a piece to the younger, and he too did not die.

After this initial ceremony the two brothers ate together happily. Having finished their first meal the sky-lady ordered the men to collect some dry wood (kangkun[72]) and to make a torch, in order to have a light on their way to the village and the beach.

The sky-lady in the lead, the three of them went and took the road named Asadares (asar-banyan, dares = sunshine) and thus they went to the villages of Saribra.

When the three emerged out of the wood with the burning torch, the villagers became frightened and they ran away hiding themselves.

The sky-princess however called upon the people, saying : "Do'not be afraid, come to me. What you see now is fire and it does not kill people".

The villagers then came out of their hiding-places and went to their houses. Because they did not know where to place the fire without burning their houses, for the third time the sky-goddess came to assist them and she gave instructions.

People had to make a fire-place : some sand or clay on a piece of tree-bark.

This was only the beginning of the support the villagers got. The sky-goddess showed them a well where they could get clear drinking-water (named Ynonga[73]).

(The last section of the myth concerns the natural birth of children, as we saw in C2, only one feature differs i.e. the name of the old man in this version is Manganaidi[74] and he cut the women from behind, not in their abdomen.)

C4. *The dancing goddess who fell from heaven*[75]

Variant, third version

(The initial part of the myth mentions the fact that the people of a certain village had no fire. The name the informant had forgotten. In this version, not two brothers, but a married couple went to the garden and had their encounter with the fire-goddess.)

On a certain day a married couple went to their garden to take some tubers, to peel them and to lay them in the sunshine, because the sun was very hot that day.

Suddenly the two heard a voice calling : "Hiya".

The couple looked around in every direction, but they saw nothing (special).

After a few moments they heard the voice of the goddess again, but this time the married couple saw her at once.

The goddess said she had fallen from heaven, because all the goddesses were dancing (and she joined them) but all of a sudden she fell to the earth and she fell together with a big piece of plank of the linggoa[76] (mahogany) kind.

At the time she fell she landed on the smaller branches and leaves of a huge banyan-tree.

The goddess descended from the tree and joined the married couple. When they had met the goddess said to the couple : "Look for some wood from the oru-tree, which is dry, we will try to make fire".

(The heavenly Lady then showed how to make a fire-drill and she performed the preparations to make fire. The first food was roasted by the goddess, but the two human beings were afraid they might die if they should eat it.)

The goddess had to use all her persuasive power to convince the two. ...

"At the time night-fall came the goddess prepared a torch, which she lit when it was completely dark. When the three of them walked to the village, the inhabitants grew very disturbed about the 'approaching danger' and they fled in every possible direction. The man then ran to his fellow villagers and appeased them, hence they came back and took over the fire".

(In this version nothing is said about birth in the natural way, but two more versions mention the combination : attaining fire and the instruction about childbirth.)

C5. *The origin of fire*[77]

In former times the inhabitants of our villages did not yet know the fire. That is why they ate their food raw, because they did not know how to cook it.

Nevertheless nobody died through lack of food, on the contrary : people got offspring and multiplied in great numbers and in rapid succession. They were all healthy and prosperous.

The history of the discovery of fire runs as follows : Once upon a time, on a certain day two people, a married couple went to their garden, which was a couple of miles away from their village.

In order to reach the garden, they had to climb a mountain first and then descend on the far side. There in the valley was their garden.

At the top of the mountain a genimu-tree[78] grew. This tree had (among many others) two big branches which came close together when the wind started to blow.

In the long run the two branches became strong and rugged, and when the wind blew hard the two branches now growing crosswise rubbed against each other.

Gradually there was a heap of scrapings below the tree. Then it happened, that through the strong wind, the two branches rubbed very strongly and fast which caused much heat. Eventually a spark of fire, and more and more of them, sprang to the scrapings which were ignited by the rain of sparks, and they took fire.

The two people on their way to the garden, came near the place where on the hilltop the genimu-tree stood. By now the flames grew higher and roared menacingly.

The two people hearing this, seeing the dense smoke billowing from the underwood and bushes, became terrible frightened. When they came nearer and saw the fire they fled in panic.

One of the habits of our people in former times was, when they saw something new and strange, they drew the conclusion this must certainly be a kind of malignant spirit or an illness on his way to attack human beings.

That was the reason why the the married couple did not have the courage to come nearer to the fire.

But, after some time, they saw the result of the burning : grass and weeds grew much better than elsewhere, and so they considered the usefulness of this new phenomenon.

They must have tried or discovered accidentally that roasted tubers were much better than raw, that voluminous tree-stumps hold the fire much longer than thin ones. So in the long run they started to make use of the fire, they even learned the technique of making fire. A new dimension was added to their human possibilities.

C6. *Fire from the sun*[79]

(Only a short note, not the myth itself is at our disposal.)

The inhabitants of Inanwatan, the Western part of the so-called Bird's head peninsula, worshipped the sun and the moon, as we will elaborate in the second volume of this series. This fact must be mentioned here, in order to understand the behaviour of the people after the fire came. The short notes run as follows :

"Fire was unknown in former times (so the people had to eat their food raw, at best sun-dried).

The bird Arosiro, a kind of the swallow species, flew all the way to the sun and took some fire from there.

At the time he fulfilled this task he was bigger than swallows usually are, they say his size could be compared to that of a pigeon.

When this big Arosiro brought the fire back from the sun, the Inanwatan-people (the Bira) became so angry, they maltreated the bird, they cursed him and spit upon him.

Through this treatment the body of the bird shrivelled so much that he became the size of the ordinary swallows we know in our time".[80]

C7. *The culture-hero Kungu and fire*

In former times there lived at the place Wombe a man named Kungu. He possessed the moon stored away in a sago-bowl. The moon was so hot Kungu was able to cook his food on it.

On a certain day Kungu went to the small lake Sangur, in the neighbourhood of the present Sengi, to prepare some sago.

He met there two sisters, who followed him and eventually became his wives.

It happened that to Kungu fire was unknown, but his two wives instructed him how to make fire.

With a small flint, a piece of bamboo and some tinder, touchwood, they made fire. (Between thumb and fore-finger the piece of flint is held underneath a bit of tinder, then one strikes hard alongside the bamboo. This "striking", creates sparks, caught by the tinder etc.)

When Kungu for the first time cooked food (roasted, grilled) and began to eat, he just had to vomit. The women however took some "bush-salt" and after that Kungu could endure to eat his food prepared in the "modern" way.

SECTION D

LIFE ON AN ADVANCED LEVEL[81]

D1. *Through the gates of the underworld*[82]

The ancestors told us, their descendants : Once upon a time people lived on the surface of this tangible world. They lived just as human beings live now. They were born, grew up into maturity, they married and became fathers and mothers. Human beings could and can create human beings out of themselves, but these human beings grew old, they withered away, but not forever.

At the end of their first life, when they had already grown old, they were able to rejuvenate themselves, just as the snakes do. Our great ancestor Manseren Mangundi was an old man indeed, but by the power obtained from the morning-star he was rejuvenated by throwing himself into the fire of an iron-wood tree. He called forth the four main-clans of the Numforese people on the holy Island of Numfor[83].

But on the same island the human beings lost the power to continue their life after sickness, death and old age.

This happened as follows :

After Mansren Mangundi had created the four clans, the houses and the inhabitants, they had no gardens but they got plenty of food, called forth by Manseren Mangundi.

Some people did not trust the words and the power of Mangundi, therefore on a certain day when they saw smoke rising from the far away island of Arwa (Japen), they asked themselves : "What have we to do next ?".

It was at that time things went wrong, because a woman of the subclan Rumbekwan named Infanduarni[84] replied to the question which was already answered by Manseren Mangundi himself : "Stay where you are, you will never have lack of food".

But this woman opened her mouth and said : "What we must do? Only one thing : Make your canoes, your paddles, and go fetch us food from the Island of Arwa".

And people did what the woman said. This was the first wrong step. The second advice given by Mangundi had been : "If somebody falls ill, even dies, do not wail, don't start to sing the mourning-song. Let me know and then you'll see what will happen".

On a certain day however a child fell ill and shortly thereafter died. The clan of the deceased was Rumbekwan and it was Infanduarni's clan. When the people in their confusion and bereavement asked : "What must we do now?" it was this same woman Infanduarndi who gave the solution, saying : "The child is dead, let us wail and mourn" (bar, kanes kajob[85], or : munabai).

Hastily Mansren Mangundi came forward and repeated once more : "(Please) don't wail about this small child. It is much better you keep silent, because the child will live again".

But the words of Infanduarndi to their people : "Wail your mourning-song, because the child has left this world behind", (made much more impression) so all the people started to wail the mourning-song (kanes kajob).

At that moment Mangundi said : "All my orders you refused to fulfil, and therefore I let you know : because you did not listen to me, the child is really dead.

These are my new orders : Take some sleeping-mats and enfold the corpse; take this rattan and bind the mats; take a piece of wood to carry the dead body, because all of you from now on have to know : "From soil the Lord made you, to soil you shall return".

And at that very moment the gates of the underworld (jenaibu, soroka) were opened, and near the entrance an old woman named Imbias[86] kept watch.

The "watchwoman" Imbiasi gives permission to enter the underworld (inside the earth and at the seabottom) on two conditions :

1. The human being who wants to enter and to live there has to show his tattoo-marks, in the shape of a + (a small cross), and the drawings of the tools their deceased parents and ancestors had used (pa).
2. The decorations the deceased was entitled to wear : feathers and a comb or a headshawl, to prove that he has been a respectable member of his group.

In the underworld all old people are rejuvenated, they gain eternal life. The first time of welfare and eternal life on the surface of this world came to an end. Now on an advanced level, liberated from the boundaries of the earthly body, life goes on forever. The dead are not really dead, with one of their two souls they live on in the ordinary world (with their nin); but with their second soul, their rur[87] which is the real man, they live in the underworld (jenaibu).

D2. *The connection between the two worlds*[88]

Serapasamai, the man from Menewar and his wife Imbarasai (were married) and Imbarasai became pregnant (for the first time). When her abdomen grew a little bit big, her mother-in-law locked her away for a short time.

She bandaged the abdomen with a man's loincloth.[89] The grandfather (to be) went to the sago-wood with his wife, and they felled a tree and, prepared the sago-flour in order to have food for the forthcoming ritual of "anbeyor" (to avoid sorrow for his grandson).

Serapasamai went hunting. He took with him a wild boar arrow, and also an ordinary arrow and he shot (with these arrows) ten wild swine, ten kangaroos and twenty birds. He brought his catch to the shore and his father and mother carried the sago home.

When the child, a son, was born her mother-in-law put mother and child in the seclusion, where they had to remain until the child became somewhat older and stronger.

Serapasamai went hunting every day and his father prepared sago.

When the child grew big enough mother and child were allowed to leave the secluded spot in their house (and they put a shell-ring on his feet).

After some time, when the shell-ring became too narrow, his father and grandfather went to the woods : hunting and sago-preparing to serve the guests at the celebration of the breaking of the first ankle shells.

(After this had happened) Serapasamai went hunting again, every day and each day he got even more results. He "shot" twenty wild swine, twenty kangaroos, and forty birds.

And this went on and on. On a certain day his father warned Serapasamai saying : "Be careful (and take it easy), for our smoked-pigs rack is full of meat". But the son replied to his father : "We have not yet much, I have to get some more".

Thus he went on hunting, and did not listen to his father who repeated every day the same warning : "Be careful, let nothing happen to you because you have a son to leave behind if you should die". On a certain day Serapasamai came home and he had fallen ill. He said to his father : "My body is ill", and he said to his mother : "Make some hot water for me, so I can have a bath, I have a touch of fever".

After he had taken his bath he said in the afternoon to his father : "(Father) I am going to die!".

His father said : "Hiye, but I said to you (the other day) you are going (hunting), but be careful. But you did not listen. I said to you : 'let us sing (using) with what we have (already) got'. But you refused saying : 'Why?' having in mind to have abundance of food for our guests, for the ceremony of the life-protecting-song.[90] Now you are dying, leaving your child".

After Serapasamai died they buried him in the evening and they made for him a bamboo-tube reaching down to his forehead.

Every morning and evening his father took water and poured it in the bamboo.

The (deceased) lay (in his grave) until all his flesh had decayed. Then his father went (to the grave) and exhumed the remains. The skull he took, brought it seawards (to his house) and placed it in his sleeping-mat.

In the morning-time the widow (of Serapasamai) carried her child on her back, but she took (also) the skull of her husband and put this in a bag which she hung over her shoulder.

In this way the two of them went to the wood watching the tawan-tree (Langsium domesticum), and in the evening they went home.

The next morning her father-in-law said to her : "It is better that the two of you go and take care of the tawan-tree, because the birds start to come and pick the fruits".

This was the way in which the days went by. Every day mother and child (with the skull in the bag) went to the woods and every nightfall they returned.

(On a certain day) the woman went to the tawan tree, carrying child and skull, but the childs father Serapasamai came from the abode of the dead and he climbed in the tawan-tree eating the fruits.

He sat in the tree-top and some fruits fell on the ground where the young woman saw them.

She cursed the birds saying : "Those damned birds, they are picking my child's fruits, that is too bad, they will finish them all".

The next day they went again and the father was already there throwing the fruits for his child to eat them.

That is why the child smelled his father and started to cry. He cried so desperately his mother was not able to appease him. The mother therefore called her younger sister : "Come hither, so you may carry my boy".

But the aunt too was not able to attract the attention of the boy. Then the boy started to speak, because he smelled his father every time they came near the tree and he said : "Mother, my father is right here". But the mother replied : "I placed your father's skull in this bag here". After that the child cried and wept in such a tumultuous way, even his aunt could not appease it, therefore she said to her sister : "This child of yours is crying too vehemently, I cannot stand it any more, this your orphan". But the mother said : "He is crying for his father".

The father, Serapasamai (heard and saw all this) and he descended a little bit lower to the ground. There he picked a whole bunch of tawan-fruits and threw them down to his child.

The mother said : "Those damned birds, they destroy all my boy's fruit, this is really to bad".

(The tale went on and on. The father came, picked more bunches of taiwan-fruits etc.)

Then the boy saw his father and said to his mother : "Look up there, there is my father". But the mother refused to believe it. She said : "It may be another man trying to deceive me".

Now the father Serapasamai descended from the tree, went to his wife and said : "Throw away that object (the skull) hide it somewhere. (Look) I am here, it is me".

But his wife replied : "No (that is not true) you are deceiving me". Her husband said : "No you are wrong, it is not true what you suspect, I am (really) your husband".

Then his wife took the skull landwards, hid it there and threw away her mourning-attire. This done she went seawards again and said to her parents-in-law : "Throw away your mourning-attire and (garments), your child and I are coming".

Serapasamai's parents (believed these words and) threw away their mourning-attire and garments, and the mother said : "All right, it is exactly as I told you when I said unto you : 'Just go landward, stay near the tawan- tree, he will certainly come out'".

Serapasamai then came out (of the wood) and stayed with his wife and child in their house (on the bank of the river). When in the night-time he slept with his wife he instructed her and said : "If they (the women) ask questions, don't answer and just stay inside (the house)".

Thus she remained inside the house for four days. Each day the women of the village called her to come out, so they could ask her some questions, but she did not come.

They called her continuously until she could not stand it anymore and then she came out to the back-premises of the house and she listened to the women.

They asked her : "Young woman, when your husband sleeps with you in the night, how is his body, is it cold?" She did not answer yet too soon, but daily this questioning went on and on hence she could not take it any more. They asked her : "Young woman, when you sleep (with your husband) what is he like? Because his body is new (tell us) is it cold?" Then Serapasamai's wife answered : "It is cold indeed".

Her husband had gone into hiding, near to them and so he could hear what was said. He was ashamed and angry and said to his wife : "Woman, you! Well, I instructed you, but you did not listen to me. I will go and leave your child and you". And he took his bow and a small arrow and descended quietly by the fore-premises of the house and left.

His wife followed him, searched for him in the river, but in vain. She said : "The man descended (from the house) he left because he is ashamed". She then took her child and carried it on her back. Wailing she cried : "My husband, you, where are you going?"

(Hearing the sound of the wailing) an old woman named Indoki spied the woman and child and asked : "Why are you wailing and crying? Take your son and let him eat of the rest of the sago-meal his father, in passing here, just ate. There is the way".

(These events went on and on. Everytime the young woman gave her gifts and asked the way her husband took. Wailing and calling her husband's name she went on and at last she arrived at the house where the old woman Indoki lived.)

Nearing the house the old woman Indoki called her saying : "Don't wail and cry anymore. Your husband is here, he lives in this house, he is sitting (near the fireplace)".

The young woman (entered the house and she) wept (for joy), and they spent the night together, but (in the middle of the night) Serapasamai said to his wife Imbarasai: "This night I am going to paddle and fish (with a torch). Take care of the fire, keep it burning and sleep until I come home. If the fire goes out let the two of you just sleep on. I shall come with the torch and we will light the fire again, but do not go to the old woman".

The wife and son however slept and the fire went out and the two became terribly cold. Then she saw Indoki sleeping and her knees glowing (like smouldering embers) and she said : "Lo, there is fire". And the wife took the fire-tongs (went to the old woman) and hit the knees of the old woman and they snapped off.

The old woman yelled (from pain) saying : "Oh, my knees; take it with you. But you will never go seawards (to the earth) again, never will you go to your father and mother (ever more).

And the (young) woman sat down until her husband came. She said to him : "The knees of the old woman I hit and they snapped off". Her husband replied : "Hiye, I said to you : 'Don't go to the old woman over there. But you did not listen. Now we do not go back seaward anymore, that is finished. We all have to remain here in the underworld (suroka) we do not go to the earth again".

The (young) woman just sat down and wailed. She cried many days, she wailed (because of the loss of) her father and mother. And the bereaved parents of the (young) woman too put on their mourning-attire and garbs for the sake of their child.

Therefore people now say : "Those who died, they went to the suroka, they came back again, but now, because

Imbarasai did not obey, she hit the knees of Indoki and they snapped off. Indoki (is the one who) prevents them. Those who die, they do not change any longer, but they merely disappear at once to the suroka.

D3. *Fun Gèm, the once open connection, blocked*[91]

Fun Gèm had died and left for the land of the dead.

At that time there still existed a road connecting the land of the living (this earth) with the land of the dead.

When Fun Gèm died he left behind his wife and her little son. She decided to go in search of Fun Gèm and she took the road leading into the country.

On her way she met some women in the sago-woods who were busy rinsing out the sago-pulp.

She asked them : "Did you see Fun Gèm pass by ?" "No we did not", they said, "but if you want to find him, just walk straight on and you will certainly arrive (at his place)."

The woman then went on for quite a distance, guiding her little boy along with her.

(On her way) she sees a woman working in a garden. "Did you see Fun Gèm pass by ?" she asked. "No I did not", said the woman," but you just keep your way straight on, and you certainly will find him".

The woman and the small boy went on and on until they met some men in the forest occupied with the chipping of a canoe. The woman asked them the same question again : "Did you see Fun Gèm passing by ?" "Yes", they said, "we did, and if you go just straight on you will arrive at a beach. On that beach there are two houses, but be careful you climb (ascend) the right one. One of the two houses is completely built of wood, if you climb into that one you will end up in the big fire. The other house is built on golden stilts (poles) and it has a golden ladder. You may safely climb into that one and you will certainly find Fun Gèm there".

The journey for the woman and her small son appeared to be long, but at last they arrived at the beach with the two houses. The houses are exactly similar, but only one of the two has indeed beautifully twisted stilts of gold and a golden ladder too. The woman and her small boy ascended that one and entering they really found Fun Gèm.

The encounter was really magnificent and they wanted to remain together forever.

About the time of nightfall Fun Gèm said : "Tonight I go fishing (with a torch). Then you will have something to eat. But bear in your mind, if it gets cold, you are not allowed to move around. Remain at your (sleeping) place. Don't try to make fire or something like that. Be careful, I have warned you. Just lie where you are and don't move".

The man then took his fishing-gear, embarked in his canoe and went away.

Mother and child laid themselves down to get some sleep. This night became pitchdark.

Suddenly the wife awakened from terrible cold. She shivered all over her body. She lifted her head and sat up and she saw in the middle of the room a smouldering fire.

The woman did not think of the warning of Fun Gèm any more. She wanted to have some fire and crawled to the middle of the house, groping through the darkness.

By means of the small glowing ember she saw, she would be able to stir up the fire again.

She grasped with her hand at the glowing ember, thinking that the ember formed the end of a piece of fire-wood.

She wanted to grip that fire-wood and she was really pulling at something, but it was no fire-wood at all. This was a leg.

(As soon as she got hold of this object) she heard a piercing shriek. The object was the leg, the ever glowing leg of Isokakwawi, the gate-keeper woman of the underworld.

Isokakwawi's feelings ran high. She chased the woman and the small boy out of the house and into the darkness. She scolded the woman at the top of her voice and cursed her relatives (from her ancestors on) : "You shall have no father anymore, you shall have no mother anymore, you shall have no brothers nor sisters anymore" and so on.

The woman and the little boy became terribly frightened. They fled into the forest. And during their flight, falling, crawling, stumbling and running, they heard a terrible noise behind them. All the (big) trees along their path toppled over.

And so it went on their whole long way back. At last they arrived at their own village.

From that time on, the way to the land of the dead has been blocked. No living being has been able to go there any more.

Children's ditty in the Dore-Bay (Manokwari) [92]

Grandmother I see him.
Whom is it (you see)?
Fun Gèm is the one who is coming.
Which Fun Gèm?
Fun Gèm, the one I killed,
The well-known, who is dead!

D4. *The maiden Aighai Rafenai and the way to heaven* [93]

Once upon a time there were two humans, a brother named Sibusinawéri and his sister Aighai Rafenai.

On a certain day the two of them went (to the wood) to prepare some sago-flour. The sun was already high and was shining brightly and the day grew hot.

After they had made five buckets Aighai Rafenai stood on the bank of a river which had very clear water. She took that water and with it rinsed the sago-pulp.

From left and right the singing of birds sounded in the trees, and their voices sounded very sweet.

Suddenly a wonderful coloured leaf floated from the air and fell exactly on the spot where Aighai Rafenai drew water to rinse the sago-pulp.

Seeing this marvellous leaf she picked it up and inserted it in her hair.

To be exact this leaf was dropped by a man from the other world. His name was Dorado Siworoka.

The brother Sibu Sinaweri came carrying a basket filled with sago-pulp which he had prepared for his sister.

Aighai Rafenai then told her brother about the beautiful leaf. He wanted to have a closer look at it, but Aighai Rafenai refused and held it tight.

In the quarrel now arising Sibu Sinaweri drew his haircomb from his hair and struck his sister so badly that Aighai Rafenai died.

After (her relatives had) wailed a couple of days, the corpse was brought into the forest and laid on a scaffolding inside a canoe screened by a fishtrap.

Two days later Dorado Siworoka descended to the earth by means of his ladder and he took a small boy along.

The two of them went hunting loris birds.

When they passed the location where Aighai Rafenai was laid Dorado Siworoka shot (with an arrow) a loris bird which fell down exactly on the scaffolding of Aighai Rafenai. Dorado (not knowing where the bird had fallen) ordered the child to go and take the bird.

Because Aighai Rafenai was a very beautiful woman and she lay there adorned with all her ornaments, the child was frightened and did not have the courage to take the bird.

(Then Dorado Siworoka came) and when he saw the corpse of the marvellous creature, his heart desired the maiden and he resuscitated her (at once).

When Aighai Rafenai became conscious she was extraordinarily amazed that she was roused from the dead and lived again.

After that Dorado Siworoka took Aighai Rafenai and ascended with her to the other world.

There was everything in abundance and nothing lacking.

Dorado Siworoka married (then and there) Aighai Rafenai. In that upperworld bananas and all kinds of foodstuff and flower-gardens could be seen; wealth was abundant[94] there[95]. At a certain time a female (sorcerer) Ghasaiwin went to that upperworld because a child had fallen ill and the Ghasaiwin wanted to give back the soul (to the child).

Then she saw Aighai Rafenai, and thought it could not be Aighai Rafenai but a woman with the same appearance.

After she had seen her two or three times she went to her and asked her about her real identity and then (she heard) it was Aighai Rafenai herself.

Everything was told now to the Ghasaiwin : her death, until her resuscitation and ascension.

This news the Ghasaiwin told to Sibu-Sinaweri, the brother of Aighai Rafenai (after she returned to the earth).

From that moment on there was a connection and communication between the two worlds and it was just wonderful.

In the mean-time Aighai Rafenai gave birth to a child, a boy. (and when the child grew) the time drew near that the boy had to be initiated and on that occasion mutual promises between the two worlds should be made.

Sibu-Sinaweri was the man who built a house (for the ritual and ceremonies). This house was made entirely of bamboo.

When the time to celebrate had come, the two worlds (and their inhabitants) started to meet each other.

The celebration-house had a very long shape and food was in plenty.

At midnight-time Sibu-Sinaweri had in mind that at the time the (inhabitants of the) two worlds should unite and express their mutual promises, the inhabitants of this world would start a brawl so Aighai Rafenai could remain on this world.

Therefore all the people (of this world) took a piece of bamboo and they started to strike (whatever was near to them) and they danced (vehemently).

All this noise and the striking and whirling earth-people confused and frightened the inhabitants of the other world, therefore they were metamorphosed into fire-flies (and flew away).

All that happened on that eventful night caused the rupture of the connection between the two worlds for ever. Aighai Rafenai and her child were taken by Dorado Siworoka (into the other world).

Nowadays there does not exist a connection any more between the dead and the living people.

NOTES

[1] This is the only text we borrowed from South New-Guinea, from the river Casuari, a tributary of the Digul-river. It is a remarkable example of a text giving an account of the Creator and the creation of the earth and man. Such an account is rare indeed, even among other well-known tribes like the Marind-Anim (cf. Van Baal 1966). They even deny the existence of a Supreme Deity, as H. Nevermann explicitly concludes : "Nie wird ein Marin-anem (sic !) sich überzeigen lassen, dass Tomarub (according to the Digul-people) der gute Herr der Toten ist, und ein Diguler wird es stets ablehnen, Dema-Sagen zu glauben" (H. Nevermann 1941:42).

The same holds true for the belief in Tefafu (our first text) about one hunderd miles to the North. The Marind do not believe in him.

The Demas we mentioned have much in common with the uaropo of the Sentani-people. Of the Demas is said the same that is stated about the uaropo : "Es gibt kaum etwas, dass ein Marin-anem alten Schlages sich nicht aus seinen Dema-Geschichten erklâren könnte..." (ibid. : 42).

About the whites they have an explanation too : "Den Unterschied der Hautfarbe erklären sich die Eingeborenen so dass sie selbst bei Nacht, die Weissen aber am Tage erschaffen wurden" (ibid. : 32).

[2] Tefafu really means deity in general. The name of this deity is Kutaiwakeremi. In the narrative the name Tefafu is used in accordance with the custom of the informants. The mentioning of the real name is avoided.

[3] The words chochi (Yair) and Kwai (Kombay) could be translated as demon. All strange things and objects, the Administration and the Mission too, are said to be originated by Tefafu of the earth, who brought with him the corpse of the child of the sea-Tefafu to the West. The inhabitants of the area in which the narrative is located, admit that Administration and Mission are more powerful than themselves, descendants of the sea-Tefafu, so they are not able to cope with that overpowering force. The resistance against the coming of Administration and Mission is for a great deal caused by the belief that Tefafu will be awakened as soon as Administration and Mission enter, and the earth will be destroyed.

[4] The location of the sleeping-place of Tefafu is not agreed upon, concerning the name. It may be that nevertheless the spot is really the same. Another variant has it that he sleeps at the source of the Aré river, a small tributary of the greater Malu river, a tributary of the Kasuari-river. It stands out nevertheless that both places are located east of the recent total tribe area, about the frontier.

[5] Heirloom : valuables inherited from the ancestors.

[6] This myth was sent to the present writer (translator) by Dirk Griffioen, missionary worker in the area near the Casuari-river in South Irian Jaya (Nw. Guinea) were he lived for a couple of years amidst the tribes under discussion here.

[7] The fairy-tale element in this myth, or the fable is remarkable and stands out clear through the manner in which it is told (I suppose, with good reasons) to small children and strangers, foreigners. The myth in the form here presented was written for me by M. W. Kaisjepo in 1953. The year before I visited the area of Biak (Wardo and surroundings) for a couple of weeks. Some older people knowing I was interested in myths and folktales, told me the fable exactly in the same version as F. J. F. van Hasselt wrote down in 1907 (printed in 1908, cf. sub Van Hasselt F. J. F., in the bibliography). While very short, the whole text is given here : "*We find the triton's shell in the sea*".

A crocodile and an iguana quarrelled about the triton's shell. The crocodile got hold of the shell and so did the iguana. But because the crocodile was much stronger than the iguana, he got the shell and took it to the sea. We still can see clearly the marks of the paws of the crocodile and the iguana.

In the "fable" told to me, while the informant showed me a triton's shell, brought with him for the occasion, only one sentence was added. Here the snake was introduced; he tempted the iguana by his flattering remark : "My ! Never before have I laid eyes on a creature as beautiful as you". Distracted by these words "She" slackened her grip and lost the fight.

[8] The Biak version is given completely in my thesis (cf. lit. list). There are a great many different versions (about at least 30). This Numfor version was written by J. Rumfabe, no date.

[9] Mostly used as "Mansren Allah", the last term borrowed from the Indonesian (Arabic) language. In former times the Mission used the term' "Mansren Nangi", supposing it meant "Lord IN Heaven". But later on it became clear it has to be translated as "Lord Sky". Mansren (seren) signifies "free man" as Inseren means "free-woman". But in the social context of the three strata in society : Mansren, common man, slave (Free man, common man and slave) gradually the name was translated, by contact with Indonesians, into Lord, later on Raja = king, nobleman.

[10] It is remarkable that the informant, J. Rumfabe, first wrote Mangundi (= He himself; mangundau = you yourself etc.) and then replaced it by Mansrenba (ba = not, no), corrected in pencil. Mangundi is an abreviation of Mansren Mangundi = The Lord himself. Mostly his name is Manarmakeri

and after the baptism by fire, or the encounter with the morning-star, Sampari (or Makmesri, or Makben = star of the pig) he is named Mansren Mangundi. But the time of this alteration of his name is never explicitly mentioned. In the village Wardo there exists a clan Maker. Hence the Wardo people claim "the old man" one of the other indications of the hero of this story, that means only the MAN (Biak : man, ar : abreviation of mansar = old man) is of the clan Maker, therefore Manarmaker. Cf. also my thesis in English translation : Koreri, 1972.

[11] Bintangur-tree. In the Biak language : Mares (Calophyllum spec.)

[12] Pinang and betelnut *the* refreshment a young man has to offer to the parents, even more to his bride to be; this meant the official proposal.

[13] Bowl made of silver, stresses the high rank of the maiden concerned.

[14] The clan Rumbekwan (the long house) branched off from the last ER Rumberpur called into being by Mangundi and was "the perfect one". The Rumberpur-er got 9 subclans at the time : Rumsajor, Rumadas, *Rumbruren*, *Rumbekwan*, *Rumfabe*, Rumbobjar, Rumaikew, Rumander and Sobjar. The sub-clans printed in italics all played an important role in the history of the Numforese, and mankind.

[15] Under the heading "the threatening of life" we will elaborate about the event merely mentioned here.

[16] Van Hasselt F. J. F. mentions he once visited the area and saw the remains (cf. Van Hasselt 1914, p. 95).

[17] kinsor = kin-sasor : grasp the enshrouded (enwrapped).

[18] Cf. New Guinea 1858, p. 155-56. In 1858 the crew of the "Etna" saw a kind of temple and made the following comments : "The old man" concerned, rejuvenated (by fire) before the four Numforese villages were created, died together with his wife and son without further offspring. Before he died he ordered the Numforese people who at that time had already multiplied and were divided in different houses, to erect (to build) an empty house collectively. In this house the ancestors were to be remembered and held in honour, by way of images or statues, ...

This is the only existing statement of the death of the old man. In all the other versions it is said that he went to the West, or they end with the remark : "...he went away".

Of the 9 subclans of the Rumberpon 5 were represented by piles (poles, stilts) carved as ancestor images.

The 5 subclans, with the names of the images drawn in 1858 in brackets, are : 1. Rumbekwan (Mansani), 2. Rumfabe (Sawari), 3. Rumander (Samfari), 4. Rumbobjar (a woman called Simbeni), 5. Rumbobjar 2e. (a woman with

8 legs, no name is mentioned) Only one of the branches (lineages) of the subclan Rumsajor (Saweni) is represented.

[19] Name of the informant and writer unknown (collection present translator).

[20] Nank : supernatural power of life usualy called mana. Persons of high rank, old age, influential foreigners are supposed to have much nank. An old man or woman may freely step over a lying or sleeping person, or may let his or her shadow fall on them. For ordinary people this is forbidden. Coming home from a voyage to Tidore, the crew and leaders of the expedition will share their nank with their relatives, by shaking their hands or rub the faces and the back and front of the people and children concerned.

[21] Informant, writer J. A. van Balen, cf. Bibliography : Windesi.

[22] Informants, writers : G. Sanadi Mandowen, and M. Wambraw, both from Biak, 1950. Collection present writer. Cf. Introduction.

[23] Uri and Pasai. Two famous men in the folklore of the Geelvinkbay. They are also known in Waropen. Cf. G. J. Held, Bibliography. The two creatures are described in different ways. Tall as giants, they were able to travel by using the islands as stepping-stones. About 70 years ago Uri was described to F. J. F. van Hasselt as the High God and creator. At that time some Geelvinkbay people had the opinion that Uri was nominated by Mangundi as his deputy at the time he decided to leave Numfor. A great number of most remarkable adventures of these two beings are told. Sometimes they act as greedy human beings, cheating and tricking men and even more women. In the Geelvinkbay area many islets are mentioned as remnants and tools, petrified into rocks and stones, of the two. At some places everything strange in shape and growth : rocks, capes, a very short coconut-tree with small nuts are named after Uri.

One would almost believe and certainly get the impression that Uri and Pasai originally were to the Geelvink bay people creator and culture-hero, but gradually got a place in the folklore in which their deeds went "ad absurdem" and the two act as funny creators and imitators. Uri then plays the role of the clever creator and Pasai, the kind soul, as a kind of "soft Johnny", but sometimes in other variants it is the reverse. This short story shows every characteristic of the two : folkheroes with every virtue and vice of human beings, but then in an enlarged scale. The figure of the trickster is well known among students in cultural anthropology since 1929 (cf. J. P. B. de Josselin de Jong : "The origin of the divine Trickster", Bibliography).

[24] The big mammals in the sea are thus explained. Notwithstanding the fact that : sea-cows (duyung), sea-horses, sea-elephants etc. are not named by these European terms. Well-known is the notion that every form of life was originally found on and in the earth.

[25] Source. sub 5.

[26] Sentani. This lake right to the South of the Davonsero-mountain (the Cyclops of the maps) is dominated by this relatively high mountain (about 3000 Meters). The Davonsero mirrors his remarkable shape, sometimes shrouded in the clouds, in the surface of the lake. Several steep paths lead over the mountain to the North, where the village of Ormu is located. Deep clefts on the Northern path look forbidding to the mountain-climbers and a whole set of myths and folktales give a clear explanation of the fears and hopes filling the hearts of the inhabitants of the surrounding villages. The "god" of the Davonsero is Dobonai (3,35). The Sentani-lake itself must in primeval times have been a bay of the South Pacific sea. Some kinds of fish, such as the saw-fish are still living in the lake.

The sources of the folktales and myths of lake Sentani are many. The present writer himself several times made an investigation, and did research-work since 1931. In the bibliography one finds the writings of P. Wirz. My own sources, from different informants, are all used in this abridged view. The last investigator, in the field of wood-carving art of the Sentani people, was Jac. Hoogerbrugge. He, an artist and painter himself, discovered some remarkable traits in the Sentani art and he compared these finds with the mythology. Striking is the dualistic pattern, represented by East end West, North-South. In his conclusion he gaves in his remarkable booklet some very valuable viewpoints. As a "layman" in the field of cultural-anthropology he presents us with more material and explanations then we ever had. The conclusions are, as a matter of fact, not final. They were never meant as such, but who, digging into the soul of human societies dares to say, that his conclusions are the only true ones. In our introduction we have said something about the problem of explanation, which will remain always tentative.

[27] Source 2, 2a. Uarofo (uaropo, waropo). A very important problem form these beings. One may call them spirits, ghosts, totem, demons and even deities. Their function is clear, not their exact circumscription. One is tempted to compare them to the Dema-beings of South-New-Guinea (cf. J. van Baal) of the Marind-Anim people, but this limits the meaning the uarofos have in Sentani and the Northern-Cyclops mountain. In summing up their function and appearance, it may be stated that the uarofos are superhuman, super-

natural, and to a certain extent irrational. But as the veil over the belief of the Sentanians, which was and is secret, is not yet lifted the possibilities to complete a kind of overall picture of the religion of the people, is still a challenge. Never was the name of their High-God mentioned. We only know that he exists in the Sentani religion and in the hearts of the inhabitants. We hope to give more details, when the "dripping" source grows into a streamlet, in the near future.

About the sources : The material from P. Wirz will be marked as (1). My own published sources as (2) the unpublished (2a), J. Hoogerbrugge as (3).

Wirz discovered the important significance of the great flat and according to him "dressed" stones (1) (Wirz 1931).

He saw them on the island of Ifar. The biggest ones were 307 and 296 cm long while they were 59 and 20 cm broad. He even saw some of them in use as stilts under the houses built above the water of the lake (1) (Wirz 1923, 2).

Wirz wrote too, the stones were only found in the central villages but the present writer saw about five in the villages Ayapo, partly submerged and others nearly completely covered. The people told some uaropo-stones could not be seen, they were buried but everyone knows these spots. These stones are sacred and no house should be built on top or over them. In latter years the Sentani medicine-men smoked their coconut husk on top of the stone when sombebody had to go to the hospital in town. This was done "in order to make the sick person well again, he needs 'the blessing' of his ancestral stone-spirit". This belief is in accordance with the function of the uaropo : they were also "tutelary spirit" or "guardian spirit" of the village (2b). The same kind of ritual had to be arranged when the men were going to hunt. The smoke of the coconut, smouldering on top of the uaropo-stone had to touch their bodies, in order to make them lucky and irrisistable. It has become clear that nearly every remarkable spot or rock, rare in shape, or caves have their uaropo. When new immigrants came to Ayapo the uaropo of the cave high above the village emerged from his dwelling-place, and was recognized as their guardian-spirit, hence the new-coming people had the courage to take that place as their home.

Sometimes men possess a uaropo, and even woman are not excluded. The Sentani people got their first fire from a female uaropo in the shape of a beautiful woman (1, 1933, 15; 3, 33). The uaropo-spirit enters into the chiefs (ondoforo) when they get hoary (grey-headed). After this happens the old men concerned act as media of the uaropo.

Not only in stones and human beings do the uaropos dwell, but also in ir vers, brooks, the lakes, snakes, crocodiles and even pigs. Every kind of fruit-tree has its own uaropo and this is the same for all kinds of fish, the natural phenomena : rain, thunderstorm, earthquakes etc. This belief is not only part of the culture of Sentani, but also of Tabati, Ormu, Tanah-Merah etc.

It was Hoogerbrugge who, in the course of some years having gained the confidence of the Sentani people, for the first time put down the real background of the "uaropo" stones (as far as the present inhabitants are concerned). He states : "The stones are named 'promise stones', set up on the place were the first human being Marweri set foot on the island Jonokon. This stone is named Oinjali and while setting up this stone Marweri promised to build a village as strong as the stone. Next to this standing stone (the male stone) lies a flat one : the wife of Oinjali. Ondowafis descended from Marwéri had to sit on top of the stone in order to became as strong as the stone" (3, 22). It seems clear to me that here is meant the supernatural power of the uarofo taking abode in the stones, male and female. Not only the story of the fire-uarofo makes this clear, but it happened once in a while, that, when no male offspring and relatives were at hand, a female became ondoforo. Counting back three generations a female named Waima became ondoforo, i.e. uarofo-possessed in the direct descending line from Mahuwé, the first uarofo who lived on earth, as the myth will narrate (3,1).

One more remark about the character of the uarofo : In the myth they are sometimes mentioned as having the power to kill. This could possibly point to black magic, but even more probably it meant : maintain the order of the universe and kill trespassers, who disturb the equilibrium of the eternal order.

[28] Ondoforo (ondofolo, ondoforo kabam = the great o., on the coastal areas called ondoafi (ondowafi) in Tabati : charsori : char = men, so(ri) group; ondoforo kendin = the small ondoforo. In former times ondoforo kabam, the great chief was indeed chief of the whole village, a descendant of the most important patriclan. The different parts of the village had an ondoforo kendin (a small ondoforo as their leader in daily life). The ondoforo-kabam was in power : he arranged every kind of ritual-celebrations; therefore he was named ceremonial chief. Descendants of the uarofos, having the power of magic, they were respected by everyone. His house has to be bigger and more beautifully decorated, his canoe also. He was allowed to have more than one wife. And, if he had only two, no common villager was allowed to take a second wife in marriage. When he arrives at the village,

all and everybody has to be quiet. No water must be thrown away, while he debarks. It could mean that somebody was urinating or defecating, which would be a great insult (1; 2 passim).

[29] Mehué. Composed from the name for sun = hu. Originated from the uarofos. Cf. the narrative about the creation of the sun.

[30] Ufoi, Ifoi (servant). Compared with the other parts of Irian (Nw. Guinea) the Sentani and Humboldt bay-people have a more or less clear-cut social system consisting of different classes and levels. The following distinction can be made.

1. Ondoforo-kabam (great) with his patriclan, aristocracy, with supernatural sanctions. Ondoforo kendin (small Ondoforo).
2. Koitero, representatives of the commons, not related to the ondoforo. Their people are the common, free people.
3. The Ufoi, ifoi. Certain individuals and patriclans in the service of the ondoforos. Possibly offspring of former slaves captured on the occasion of raids in the past. Their duty is:
   a. Leaders of war-and raid-groups.
   b. Servants of the ondoforos. They have not only to work, but are important messangers and go-between in all important events. There seems to be a specialisation : The tasks are shared : hunting, warfare, negotiations, fishing, agriculture.
   c. The wives of the ufois have to do the fishing, garden-work, preparing the sago-meals. A small part is given for their own use.
   d. The ufoi are in a certain way "treasure-keepers" on behalf of their masters, the ondoforos.
   e. They have to keep an eye on every kind of work and business, even to watch carefully the behaviour of the wives of their master (1; 2. Halie, cf. Bibliography).

[31] Source 2 and 3.

[32] First heavenly village, 3, 17.

[33] In the opinion of the Sentani-people North means heaven, South means earth. As the lake is located just South of the huge Davonsero Mountain, their lake was earth and south. A journey to the South, where the rattan was cut, meant the same as : descending to the earth.

[34] Asei (Wirz, Osei) this narrative is common knowledge. To be found in all sources (1, 2, 2a, 3).

[35] The same holds true for the snake Yabero. Cf. sub I.

[36] Sources 2a and 3.

[37] Sources 2a and 3.

[38] Sources 2a and 3.

[39] Wearing decorations and adornments not according to one's rank meant : anticipation and pride and name which not could be proved. Having these, using the exact prescribed decoration, was the same as : being in power, a proof of ones status. Misuse is regarded as a serious tresspass against the existing order, and could be, and as a matter of fact has been many tim es a "casus belli".

[40] The turbulent history, embedded in legendary-myth is elaborately told by Hoogerbrugge. The most remarkable fact shown clearly in this narrative is the heterogeneous interests, the clash between neighbours, even relatives. The close-knit entity, the peaceful coexistence in a well-integrated culture-pattern seems, as far as Sentani is concerned, a Utopia indeed. The same is true of the Geelvink bay. Intertribal. inter-group-wars were frequent.

[41] The source 2a. Informants of the village of Ormu, belonging to the patriclans Nere and Jakadewa. Most of them were grey-beards. Some young relatives were listening and enjoyed the narrative they heard.

[42] See note 41.

[43] Remarkable is the fact that the inhabitants have much more elaborated their stories and tales and myth about the moon than the ones about the sun. The Sentani and Humboldtbay people know many more names for the stars and the heavenly bodies than the inland people. Cf. K. W. Galis 1955 passim (especially p. 160 etc.) and id. 1956a and 1956b. In these two studies the difference is clear. Mostly however we know very little about the observation of "the heavens" by the inhabitants because it is not always investigated carefully. This is deplorable because most informants who really know quite a few are of great age, if there are still any to be found, which is doubtful.

[44] Source : J. Hoogerbrugge 1967, p. 34-37. Id., manuscript F. C. Kamma.

[45] Cf. K. W. Galis 1956a.

[46] A classical example of the deeds and "crimes" of a culture-hero. Only a fragment is given. Cf. the whole tale Galis 1956b, pp. 46-53. Some more fragments concerning our topic will be selected. Cf. Sangrar and the incomplete men; applying of fire e. th.

[47] Ibid.

[48] Source : Warokawamer P. from Japen.

[49] "dirty", concerning the menstruation is mostly formulated as such, but this is not literally meant. The expression "moon-dirt" (mamás paik) indicates the monthly contagious situation which is dangerous for everybody, but the worst for males. Among some of the Irian tribes near the living-houses

a small menstruation-cabin is built. Mostly birth takes place in them as well. Blood is sacred, therefore taboo. Where-ever the blood of a relative is shed, the Biak-Numfor people of the same kin are not allowed to set foot on that piece of land, island, hill, mountain etc. Therefore with the maiden whose menstruation did not end, the whole community, her own family to begin with, was endangered.

50 Sang ori (the honoured moon). Sang, a word borrowed from the Indonesian-Sanskrit language. In Biak the term is : Mansren (manseren), Lord, the male variant, nobleman.

51 Dang Bulan, ibid. Biak : Inseren. Dang the female variant : Lady, noble-woman. These titles and the meaning ascribed to them clearly show the influence of the Indonesian culture. The Indonesians on their part were influenced by the Indians in their feudal systems, their dynasties and Sultanates, even in their wayang and folklore-plays. These institutions, by way of the ever-continuing acculturation-processes, were in the long run firmly established in the Ternate and Tidorese culture, from whence the Irianese were in their turn influenced in the course of time. The result of this acculturation is mostly encountered in the coastal areas. In the far-Eastern parts however, as we saw in the Humboldt bay cultures, an indigenous dynasty of a semi-feudal system developed without influence from Indonesia. The same holds good for this form of hierarchy in Polynesian societies.

52 Sources : F. J. F. van Hasselt, Galis 1955. Kamma, collection.

53 Sup (land) Tabi (the sun) : land of the sun, known by the Geelvink bay and mentioned in their myths. This name indicated not only the Jotefa- and Humboldt bay people, but the coastal area, from Tanah Merah (West of mount Cyclops) to the Humboldt bay as well. However the Jotefabay culture has its influences, by way of their kin, far over the border, deep into the Territory of New-Guinea.

54 Spirits. In the Jotefa-bay or the Tabi language they use nearly the same word as Sentani-people do, namely : ureb warefo (Sentani : uarofo).

55 Cf. the myth about the Sentani-people emerging out of the earth and the Tabati-spirit woman, who hearing the sound of the drum, went thither. She also, after having given birth to children, went back to her place of origin.

56 Informant, writer B. Mansawan, Wandammen. Collection F.C.K.

57 The Irianese (Papuans) never curse and swear by using the name of their High God. The use of his name (Nangi and Sjen in the Geelvinck bay) is strictly limited to prayers and oath-taking. "Bad language" in daily life is mostly concerned with erotic behaviour and privates. In using "strong

language" the ancestor-spirits (souls) karwar, korwar are mentioned i.e. karwaro-o, karwar-kakuye : real karwar. Good heavens is not, but : good-gracious seems therefore the appropiate translation.

[58] Wealth; here is meant the ceremonial wealth, used in ceremonial exchange (on the occasion of betrothal, wedding, birth,) and all the phases of the life-cyclus, fines, in short : the whole of social life, in cooperation as well as in competition.

It is therefore that this wealth, nearly always mentioned means : robenai = possessions, or derived from the Indonesians : arta, harta, arasa etc. The word mas-kawin (bride-wealth) is used too. Mas = gold, kawin = marriage in Indonesian.

The moon as the source of wealth, in the above-mentioned sense is an ever-recurring theme in myth and folk-tales. About the relation between moon and pig we will elaborate later. The symbolic meaning of this animal and the moon is obvious.

[59] Source. Informant, writer J. Paprindey, 1950. Collection F.C.K. Cf. too G. J. Held, 1956, p. 285. Here is given a quite different version. The informant was of the village of Waren. Paprindey came from the scene of the event itself.

[60] The sea and land mammals here referred to, are indeed the totem-animals of the Humboldt bay-people. All of them are mentioned in Galis 1955, p. 132-33. To be exact : thirteen species.

[61] The first part the "background" is from memory (cf. abreviation in Kamma 1954, p. 68) 1972, p. 70). The information in writing got lost during world war II. Kijne however refers to the text he once probably had in his book "Effata" 1960, p. 11 and 22. The text is from the collection of the late F. J. F. van Hasselt, written down about 1925-1930 by Petrus Wandow.

[62] The estimation of the time passed by since the origin of fire amounts to ca 400.000 years. One look at the myths of the tribes of Irian Jaya (New Guinea) makes it clear at once that many of the tribes have a tale (myth) about the origin of fire in their tribe or village. Must we accept the theory that no diffusion from the culture-complex, which the technics of the making of fire certainly is, took place to "the ends of the earth"? Each culture-province (area) would in that case have developed, in a more or less spontaneous way, its own solution. Another possibility however seems more likely, though we are not able to prove it, i.e. "each tribe has the inclination to develop their own theory concerning the origin of certain phenomena". Sanctioned by the realm of the supernatural these myths had obviously impressed members of other units. Until recent times these aetiological

explanations formed an important part of the folklore of a given tribe, area, clan or even an individual. In our introduction we mentioned this fact in a wider context.

About fire it can be said, that the inhabitants of Irian (Nw. Guinea) had no volcanoes in their area. There was a time, about the 6th decennium of the 19th century, that the opinion was held the Arfak-mountain was" a sleeping volcano" but the proof could not be given. Remarkable is the fact, that together with the obtaining or the discovery of fire, natural childbirth was taught to the people. Fire and life were therefore closely connected.

Before World War II I wrote down a myth of the Biak people about human beings not knowing the use of fire, but they ate charcoal (sic) !. Only I, as a stranger, was astonished at this contradictory element in the myth. The question whence this charcoal came was never put. Source Hoogerbrugge 1967, 39.

[63] The translation "goddess" is arbitrary. Sentani people mentioned uarofo's meaning in general : spirits, demons (of a benign and malignant character). Sometimes one is inclined to translate gods (goddesses).

Wirz (1933) in a quite different version said : "Auch Feuer besassen sie noch nicht. Dies erhielten sie aber erst später, von einer andern Frau, einem Uarópo (Geist) ... ", p. 21.

[64] Withcraft. This may have the meaning of the use of the power of a malignant spirit, Uarofo, and belongs to the same class as the benignant uarofo. This character watches the transgressing of the rules laid down by the ancestors, or the uarofos.

[65] Wirz used in this context the expression "vergewaltigen" (rape) which seems to be correct, but, compared to the background of this myth, is very unlikely. Cf. Wirz 1933, p. 21.

[66] Informant, writer I. Rumaropen, from Padaido. Out of 5 different versions of this myth at my disposal four of them mentioned the gift of fire and the instruction about child-birth in the natural way. The differences are important, the more so in this time as the scholar Levy-Strauss elaborates broadly about the meaning of these differences. Only a few remarks will be added to what is said in the introduction. Historical *factors* play an important role. The diachronical element in the myth, i.e. the depth of time ,is clearly shown in the historical influences at work in the mind of the myth-tellers. In the versions here presented the time-factor is of utmost importance.

Remarkable is the fact that the owners of the myth, the tellers too, take for granted that the caesarian section is applied. Never is mention made of the possibility of sewing up the womb, while in other circumstances they try to mend whenever possible. This is probably one of the myth-elements. Human beings are powerless, dependent. One gets the impression that "the old man" (the master-cutter) is not a normal human being. He lives on his own, his solitary life is abnormal. In the mythical situation men play a role, but after the natural birth is introduced every male is tabooed away. Assistance on the occasion of childbirth is the exclusive task of older females. In fact it is one of the secrets of life, which solution males could not find.

[67] The two words : ripe and cooked are used in a rather different connotation then the English and European languages have. Ripe (myas; everything, fruits etc. which grew solid and dry are named "dry". Indonesian : kering. Biak : myas, pnas. The last word is applied to older people too). All kinds of fruit, everything which grew soft is called : mbrai; the same word is used for cooked food : mbrai, Indon. : masak).

[60] Inseren (Insren) Nankri (Nangi). Inseren = Lady, noblewoman, princess, goddess) against Mans(e)ren Nangi (Lord Sky). Nangi = exactly *sky*, but in modern times heaven. It does nevertheless not mean : the abode of the dead. In the myths it always indicates : the abode of supernatural powers, but cf. the introduction, about the layers (strata of the universe).

[69] The variants in the myths about fire are concerned with the names of beings and places. This may be due to the different character of the narrators, their memories, even more their way of presenting the events. Some have a more matter-of-fact style, others like to elaborate, even moralize. When given the plain facts the outsider usually does not understand. Much information is taken for granted, it is obvious.

[70] Inèki (in : woman; èk = i dèk : she climbed; i = it). In everyday language one would say : The tree the woman climbed (it) Aiknam in-ya-dèk-i.

[71] marpjan-tree (mar = loincloth). Formerly the loincloth of the men was made from the bark of the mar-tree.

[72] Kangkun (kun = to enflame). Kangkun = cooking, i.e. preparing a meal by roasting, grilling, cooking.

[73] Inonga. In = bin, woman.

[74] Manganaidi (composition of different words. Man = male; mangan = eagle, di (ri) = (s)he. The whole however seems mysterious, people know who is indicated by this name, but the real meaning is unknown.

[75] The dancing goddess. Informant N. Rumbiak. The dancing of heavenly beings is mentioned also in G. J. Held 1956, p. 368. In Waropen it is "the woman from the moon (who fell on the earth) who brought fire to the earth".

[76] linggoa-wood. The plank brought by the goddess had a red aspect, and flaming grain composition. The Biak word is naswaren.

[77] Informant Amos Bebari. N. Japen. One of the two texts (the second is from Biak) where the spontaneous outburst of fire took place by way of friction between two tree-branches. The supernatural element is totally absent here.

[78] Genimu-tree. Well-known because the leaf-sheath of the flower consists of black, waterproof fibre.

[79] Cf. Adatrechtbundel XLV Nieuw-Guinea 1955, p. 179.

[80] The impertinence of the swallow aroused the anger of the inhabitants, because the sun is worshipped in Inanwatan as their high-god.

[81] This title is in reality a kind of conclusion, drawn by the present writer out of a great many discussions and in an abbreviated form given by the informant J. Rumfabe. At the time of our last encounter he was a grey-beard of a proximately 80 years of age. As he was a member of one of the most outstanding clans of the Doré (Bay) it seemed appropriate I laid in his mouth, what he never wrote down, but certainly would have approved. The readers are requested to take my word for it. The dead are not really dead, but live in an other-worldly situation. How this situation is supposed to be is laid down in several myths we selected out of many of this kind.

[82] Underworld. Mentioned in a great many texts (forthcoming also in a publication on "Biak Numforese texts".) The inhabitants do not use the circumscription : underworld. They call it "suroka" (soroga, etc.) after the Indonesian word surga, which means heaven, but then in a christian or moslemic way. The Biak and Geelvinkbay-people use the words : jenaibu, snonaibu. Jen = beach; snon = man; aibu = soul of the dead. There are always two even three locations mentioned : 1. Inside the earth. 2 : On the sea-bed. 3. In the sky. The last possibility may have been introduced in the local mythology as a result of acculturation with the West (Indonesia, Asia, Europe).The informant (writen and oral tradition) was Jan Rumfabe.

[83] Numfor (Num = nus = island; for = sacred, taboo, fire). The meaning and significanse of this island is very important, as was and is also the island Meosbefondi (Meos = island; for = holy, taboo; befor = being for. The result of this analysis is : it has the same meaning as Numfor.

[84] Infanduarni (Infandwarndi). In = woman, fa = causes; duarn = stir, mix up). The woman who confuses everything. The word dwarn means really "stirring of the surface of the water". Cf. Van Hasselt dictionary sub verbo (i = he or she; always at the end of a word composition).

[85] disen kayob (sing mournsong). Usually it is said : kanes kayob = weep or cry the kayob. The sentence really runs as follows : i bjé wer ko kanes kayob = it is much better we wail (weep) the kayob.

[86] Imbias = In, influenced by the following consonant b the n becomes a m. bas = to open; byas, bias = she, he, as infix. The whole word is = The woman who opens.

[87] nin and rur. Nin = shadow = soul; rur = soul, the innermost, juice; f.i. srai-rur = juice of the coconut, but also : boiling water : rur i sai = the water is boiling. It is never allowed to step on someone's shadow. Mirror = fa-nin = causing the shadow.

[88] Cf. Van Balen, Ja. A. 1915, p. 506.

[89] Dress the abdomen of a pregnant woman in order to stimulate the embryo to become a boy.

[90] Let us sing = let us perform the ritual of the breaking of the leg-decoration within the circle of dancing men and women. Sing and dance meant : disen wark = by singing, begging the assistance of the ancestors. This is one of the several phases of the initiation-cycle. Abundance of food has the aims : 1. To obtain prestige for the father and his clan. 2. A magic purpose = giving food in abundance is : spending life and promoting life for the child still in the womb, and for the community as a whole.

[91] Informant. The late I. S. Kijne who heard this myth as it was told to an elder person about the year 1916. This man was the informant who told this myth in the language of the Island of Roon.

Fun : this title means Lord. The word is used in the Raja Empat islands (Sorong and surroundings). Fun Nah = The Lord God. Naha : in the southern part of Sorong (Seget) means : wind, storm.

[92] Children's ditty, from the Doré-Bay. Cf. Van Hasselt F. J. F., 1908 p. 585.

[93] An anonymous young pupil of the teacher training college, who came originally from Waropen, put this myth into writing. Cf. G. J. Held, 1956, "Waropense Teksten" p. 230, 364 gave totally different versions of this myth. His versions "194. Aighei Rafenai has contact (cohabits) with the dead Seraghombarokui". and the text number 195 "Aighei Rafenai" has the same tendency, but the plot is quite different. Therefore the version given in our text is important. The problem about the contact between the two worlds is more logically presented. Aighai (Held writes Aighei) means: mythical woman, primeval woman (cf. Held 1942, list of Waropen words, sub verbum), plays an important role in Waropen mythology. Nineteen times

she is mentioned as a title of a text and no less than about 80 times she plays a considerable part. (Cf. Held 1956 "Waropen texts.")

Not all the names can be analysed. Most names have older elements not known by the Waropen people any-more.

[94] Ghasaiwin. The woman-shaman, doctoress. She is able according to the Waropen people to plead with the supernatural powers, to yield a soul they have already in their power. Cf. Held "Papua's of Waropen" 1947, p. 237, etc.

[95] Wealth, valuables, exactly : possessions : the ceremonial exchange currency. Important in social contact and the functioning of all socio-religious activity. In Indonesian : mas, harta kawin : gold, valuable, bride wealth.

LIST OF IRIANESE (PAPUAN) WORDS

(S) after a word means Sentani language
(W) after a word means Windèsi language
(Wa) after a word means Waropen language
(J) after a word means Jotefa language
All other words, without indication, are Biak-Numforese ones

Abar-people (S) : giants of the village of Abar
Adama : boy, child of the lizzard according to the Jair-tribe, on the banks of a tributary of the Digul-river
adèf : sea snake
ahakai Yoble (S) : primeval snake
aibu : soul of the dead
Ajau (S) : island of, in the centre of the Sentani area, island of origin.
Ambér : stranger; amber- : styrax (yellow resin)
Amori (W) : kangaroo
anbeyor (W) : eat in order to require, celebration
—one of the ceremonials of the initiation-cyclus
anch : life-symbol (of the Egyptians)
Angradifu : at the trunk of the lime-tree. Patriclan of the Nuforese
Arosiro : swallowbird (among the Inanwatanpeople)
Arwa : island of, on the maps : Japen, in the Geelvinkbay
Asar-Asarknam : banyan-tree
Asis-mambur : comb of birds feathers = the hero's comb
Aswir : fire drill
Atasa (S) : prominent and outstanding chief among the ondoforo's

Baken : body, (land of) origin.
bar : bar doja = start to sing a song; bar = rwar, rbar : part, direction
bangka (S) : empty
Barero; Boirero (S) : chief of the Uarofo
Beba : great, important
Biak : rising up (out of the sea); Sup i Biak : Land arises
Bintangur : Indonesian name for the Biak *mares*, tree and fruit
bi-sexual : human beings in Wenggi
buma (S) : above, heaven

Charsori (J) : noble-chief (char : man, sori : many people)
Chochu : river, tributary of the river Digul, South-Irian (Nw. Guinea)

Dahaya (S) : chief (ondoforo) of the Taimé-clan
dares : sunshine, heat of the sun
Dimara : Gimalaha (Tidorese word meaning : village chief)
Dohor (J) : first human child
Doré : bay
Dunia : world (Indonesian word, borrowed by all tribes)

Efama : daughter of the lizzard (Jair-tribe, cf. Adama, both names borrowed from the Bible
embai (S) : one
Er : primeval patriclan from Numfor, cf. the four primeval Er

Fak : name of a conglomerate of different tribes near the Arfak mountain. Faksi : the Arfak-people i.e. Mejach, Manikion, Moiré, Arfoe, Mansibaber etc.
Faknik : evil spirit, ghost, power, always malignant
Fanin : mirror; nin : soul, shadow
Farimamfawar : in order to see the end of it ;farewell.
fat : four. Malucan word, used in the Raja Empat (Kolano Fat) the four chiefs or kings; cf. Kolano, korano
fi : sago porridge (S)
Fun : Lord, gentleman, Fun Nah : The Lord Wind (Moi-language, near Sorong) Borrowed from there

Gem, Kem : island of Gebé (Area of Sorong) belonging to Halmahéra
Genimu : fibre of a kind of palm-frond, used as ropes and as sieve to rinse the flour out of the sago-pulp
Ghawachu (S) : gha = twilight; wachu : drum

Halmahéra : mother of the Island. Island in Indonesia.
Hobobwe (S) : petrified rafts south of the village of Yoka (S)

i (S) : fire
Ifalo (S) : Western wind
Ifar (S) : village of the centre of Sentani
Imbias : woman who opens, the one who watches, guards

Inarjori : cape at the island of Numfor : the woman is there
Inuri : woman of Uri (Ori : sun ?), Name of the big snake
Inseren Nangi : the maiden (from) heaven, sky = the heavenly maiden
Infadwarni : woman who stirs it
Inggoirosa (W) : mountaingod Ingoi
Insoraki : woman joining the raid, name of the wife of Mangundi
Insren Nangi : Virgin, Lady of heaven
Iria (J) : land of the living

Jair : tribe near the sources of Digul-river
Jan : red fruit of the pandanus-tree
Jawisibusu : tributary of Digul-river
Jebeui : a cape in lake Sentani
Jenaibu : heaven, really; jen : beach; aibu : the dead
Jep : big seasnake
Jewaoke (S) : big tree
Jochu (S) : dog

Kais : octopus
Kamer : one of the main clans of the Numfor-Interior
Kanes : weep, mourn; kanes kajob : weep the mourning-song
Kani (S) : earth
Kangkun : to burn, cook food, roast id
Karabas : sea-snake (smaller one)
Karwaro : My ! soul of the dead, exclamation of embarrassment, anger
Kasip : iguana, hourshaped drum
Kasuari : bird of cassowari
Kawyan : one of the primeval clans of the Numfor-Interior
Kbur : triton's shell
Kendin (S) : small
Kolano, korano : Tidorese word, districts-chief, later : village-chief
Kombai : tribe in Digul area
Konori : son of Manarmakeri, Mansren Manggundi; Kon : remain; ori : sun
Korano : cf. kolano
Kwai : chochi; tributary of Digul river

Linggoa : mahogany-wood (Indonesian). Biak : naswaren

Mahowe (S) : primeval father
Maiwa (S) : snake of heaven
Mambri : hero
Mandep : cloud(s)
Manekion or Manikion : Arfak-tribe
Mangroder : frog
Mangundi : he himself

Manokwari : Menu = village; kwar : old, already
Mansanak : the splitter
Manseren (Mansren) : Lord, Free-man
Manserenba : no Lord
Manseren Mangundi : the Lord Himself. Name of folk-hero after his baptism by fire and rejuvenation
Manwen : witch, evil spirit
Maoka (S) : bracelet of plaited rattan
Marbin : loincloth for women, tree, whence the bark for the loincloth is taken
Marpjan : tree; mar : dead; pjan : easy
Marweri (S) : loincloth-wearing male
Mbrai : ripe (soft), cooked
Meach (S) : second human child
Mehuwe : cf. Mahue
Mele (S) : red coloured earth, clay
Melebu (S) : coconut oil
Meokwundi : Meos (island) ko (we) bur (left) i (it). Island in the Padaido group, near Biak
Meosbefondi : (meos-befor) : holy, taboo; i-ndi : The holy or tabooed Island
Meos Indi : fish island, near Biak
Meoskarwar : the same as Meosbefondi. Karwar : souls of the dead
Meosrifu : Island Geelvinkbay; ri fu = di fuar : the origin, trunk
Mias : ripe (hard, dry as a coconut); sterile, barren
Mié (S) : woman
Mumuchai : clan of the Jair tribe, South Nw. Guinea (Irian)
Munabai : mourning-song; abai = coffin

Nank : Power, mana, sometimes : Sky, Heaven. Nank i mjun : it rains i.e. Nank strikes; mjun = he strikes. I miun = it rains
Nangi : Sky, Firmament, arch of the Sky. Lord Sky
Napirem : nephew, fabroso (father brothers son)

Nin : shadow, soul
Ningai : Wife of Mansren Mangundi
Njan : way, path, manner, solution
Numaditj (J) : house of the living
Numberpon : Rumberpon = the first : bepon, num = rum : house. The first primeval house, clan, of the Numforese, created bu Mangundi
Numfor : holy, taboo-Island. Num = nus : meos = island. For : taboo, holy

Ondoafo (S) : traditional, semi-feudal chief
— kabam : Great, outstanding Ondoafo
— kendin : small, ordinary Ondoafo
Ondoforo : cf. ondoafo. Named in this way in the coastal area
Oransbari : Oran : a small river East Birds Head; sbari : mouth, cape near the "mouth" of a river
Orkersbari : Orkers cape. Or : sun : kér : a little bit, Cape at Numfor
Oru : tree, whose branches burn while they are still green

Pa : tattoo (marks of)
Pakriki : the solid one, village at Numfor (the first village there)
Papon sarak : bowl of silver; sarak = silver.
Pasai : legendary brother of culture-hero Uri.
Poiru : = for rjur : fire collects, assembles. Oldest name for Numfor.
Pulende (S) : navel

Resea (Wa) : soul
Ria, Lia (J) : land of the living
Robenai : possessions, wealth, ceremonial exchange valuables : Geelv. Bay
Rosa (Wa) : soul
Rumansra : house-eat-coconut = the house of the coconuteaters. One of the main patriclans (cf. er) of Numfor
Rumbekwan : long house. One of the lineages of the main four er
Rumbepur : the last house. The fourth in succession of created houses, with the meaning : the perfect clan, according to the informant
Rumfabe : house of the quarrel. Lineage of Rumberpurclan.
Rumser : house of the sago-wood. Lineage of a main clan.
Rur : soul. spirit

Sakon : they stay also (name of small seasnakes)
Samfar : bracelet of trachinis shell
Sampari = Samfari : Morningstar
Sawari Rumfabe : Primeval father of the Rumfabe lineage
Sengadji : district-chief. Tidorese word, title introduced from there
Sjari : village East Coast Bird's Head
Sneber : Sternpart of a canoe, with woodcarvings and clan-symbols
Snonkaku : Human being, man, men. Snon : nose = name; kaku : real.
Sup : land; sup ma swan : the earth; swan = sea
Suroka : dwellingplace of the dead, heaven. Derived from the Indonesian surga : heaven
Swan : sea; ra swan : go fishing; cf. sup.

Tab (J) : sun, god
Tagiob : place in the upper-Digul
Taime (S) : tree, patriclan in Sentani, mountain people (originally)
Tariaku (S) : female uarofo
Tawan (W) : tree with bunches of fruit; langsium domesticum
Tefafu : deity (in general) among the Jair people. South Nw. Guinea
Terai : baked clay-pot

Uarofo (S) : spirit, ghost, power (supernatural)
Uarofoï (S) : fire (i) uarofo
Ufoi (S) : servant, group, social stratum in the social structure of Sentani
Uri : Ori (?) = sun. Culture-hero of the Geelvinkbay

Vamini : area in the upper-Digul, South-Nw. Guinea

Wai (J) : clouds, canoe, dug-out in the Geelvink bay
Wam : wind
Wariab : village on the East-Coast of the Birds Head
Warido (S) : village on the Island of Biak and elsewhere. War : water; dori : inside of. A small river, a brook get this name also
Warofo Boiro (S) : chief of the spirits
Warowo = warofo = uarofo, cf. sub verbum
Wiwibunacho (S) : clan in Sentani
Wongor : crocodile, hero-name in Biak

Yabero (S) : primeval snake
Yasi (S) : morning-star
Yatji (J) : brother of the sun-god Tab
Yewun : primeval patriclan in Numfor
Yo (S) : village
Yoko (S) : section of a village
Yowake (S) : banyan-tree